Elite!

Elite!

The Secret to Exceptional Leadership and Performance

Floyd Woodrow and Simon Acland

First published 2012 by Elliott and Thompson Limited
27 John Street, London WC1N 2BX
www.eandtbooks.com

ISBN: 978-1-908739-45-2

Text © Simon Acland and Floyd Woodrow 2012

Extract from *British Defence Doctrine* (pp. 234–5) reproduced
by kind permission of the Ministry of Defence

9 8 7 6 5 4 3 2

A CIP catalogue record for this book is available
from the British Library.

Printed and bound in the UK by TJ International Ltd, Cornwall, PL28 8RW

Typeset by PDQ Media

Illustrations by Tilly Crawley

Extract on page 145 © Patrick Lencioni, *The Five Dysfunctions of a Team: A
leadership fable* (San Francisco, CA: Jossey Bass, 2002)
Extracts on pages 201, 203,205 © Jim Collins, *Good to Great: Why some companies
make the leap … and others don't* (New York: Random House Business, 2001)
Every effort has been made to trace copyright holders for extracts used within
this book. Where this has not been possible, the publisher will be pleased to
credit them in future editions.

I have always been fascinated by individuals, teams and organisations that truly perform at the highest levels. I have worked alongside some extremely talented people, and there is no doubt in my mind that there are core principles that weave their way like a golden thread through the minds, bodies and behaviours of those exceptional individuals. As I have discovered these principles, I have wondered why they had not been taught to me at a much earlier age. In this book, I highlight the elements which have had the most impact on my life and which remain a constant feature of the teams and organisations that truly perform at an elite level.

Floyd Woodrow

PRAISE FOR *ELITE*!

"Floyd offers an insightful and inspirational guide to leadership and team building at the highest levels."
Sean Fitzpatrick, former New Zealand All Blacks captain

"Floyd is a game-changer, able to create successful teams and environments that pursue excellence. I value the advice he gives and commend this book to you."
Andy Flower, England cricket coach

"Having had the privilege of getting to know Floyd Woodrow over the past eight years, I am not surprised that he and Simon Acland have written such a superb book, which will help others understand the skills and attitudes that are needed to be a great leader and team player. I was gripped with the fictional tale, based on Floyd's experience working in the SAS, and appreciated how the writers skilfully wove relevant personal experience into the text, to help the reader grasp the underlying concepts of elite leadership. The book's greatness lies in its authenticity: there is a complete match between Floyd the man and what he is writing about. I have no hesitation in commending Elite as an essential read for anyone who wants to understand the secret to exceptional leadership and performance."
Dr Neil Hawkes
Founder, International Values Education Trust (IVET)

"A compelling read that is a mirror image of the author – insightful, imaginative and, without a doubt, inspirational."
Bernard Hogan-Howe
Metropolitan Police Commissioner

"Floyd Woodrow hasn't just talked the talk, he's fought it. These are real life lessons drawn from the heat of the moment, prepared for in advance. That's what makes this book special."

Roger Lewis
Group Chief Executive, Welsh Rugby Union

"I have come to know Floyd Woodrow well through the valuable work he has undertaken with me and my leadership team in BT Global Services UK. As a Gartner Magic Quadrant player in global telecommunications markets we can only maintain our position of global leadership within our industry by being the best at what we do. This also means leading ourselves, each other and our people, not just to be the best, but to redefine what being the best means. This is what Floyd helps us to do. Like Floyd and Simon Acland, we also come from contrasting backgrounds and have followed different paths on our journeys to where we are now. With Floyd's help we have learned to understand ourselves and each other and to harness our strengths as individuals and teams to both achieve and stretch our objectives. This book is not a replacement for having Floyd beside you; but for those interested in his unique approach, it provides a clear understanding of the critical link he draws between personal performance and leadership. I recommend the book highly and would encourage both senior and middle managers to learn the lessons it offers in how to lead and contribute to high-performing leadership teams."

Emer Timmons
President, BT Global Services UK

"Combining front-line experience and detailed research, this is an excellent guide on leadership and building successful teams."

Gregor Townsend MBE
Head Coach, Glasgow Warriors

Acknowledgements

There are a number of people I must thank in the writing of this book:

Dr Rob Kennett, one of the world's best negotiators; Richard Cross, who has helped me understand the entrepreneurial side of leadership; and of course Simon Acland, who has been a great foil to test my theories on leadership.

I would also like to thank KM, BM, SJ, VO, MC-S, RP, JS, CT, AF, MV, ST, GL, SW, NH, and RL, who are outstanding examples of military, police, sporting and business leaders.

Finally, of course my family: my wife Sue and our wonderful children, Joe, Rhiannon and Rosie, who have been there to support, challenge and inspire me, and continue to do so.

I would also like to add an extra thank you to my son Joe, who has been instrumental in making sure I stay in the red zone.

Floyd Woodrow

Contents

Introduction   Floyd Woodrow and why you should
read this book   1

Chapter One   The magnificent workings of the human brain   5

Chapter Two   Personality types   25

Chapter Three   The North Star: understanding your own
priorities, aims and objectives   51

Chapter Four   Communication and negotiation   73

Chapter Five   Training yourself: getting into the flow   107

Chapter Six   You as part of a team   139

Chapter Seven   You as a team leader   161

Chapter Eight   You as an organisational leader   197

Chapter Nine   Conclusions   217

Appendix I   Personality profiling questionnaires available
online   223

Appendix II   The British Army's *Principles of War*   224

Appendix III   Further reading   226

Introduction

FLOYD WOODROW AND WHY YOU SHOULD READ THIS BOOK

This is Floyd Woodrow's book. It is built on his wisdom and experience. His are the stories that illustrate it, his the anecdotes that enliven it. My role has been to pull some of the words together, but I will have failed in that task unless it is Floyd's voice that comes through in those words.

Except in this introduction, that is, because here this is me speaking, Simon Acland. There are two reasons for this: first, because I can introduce Floyd and say things about him which his natural modesty would prevent, and, second, because I want to explain why my own career would have been more successful if I had known thirty years ago what I now know from working on this book.

When Floyd was a boy he developed an unswerving ambition to join the Paratroopers. He could have excelled as a professional sportsman in many fields: boxing, rugby, rowing and others too. He has the necessary physique, the determination, the desire to win, the ability to practise relentlessly in the pursuit of excellence. If he had chosen this course, I am sure that he would now be a household name.

Instead he chose the Paras, for the simple reason that he believed that this was the career that posed the greatest challenges. It was more dangerous, more demanding and more arduous in many different ways. He felt that it would stretch him most. Aged eighteen, he did so well in his entrance tests that the Army tried to persuade him to join in a different role – as an officer or an engineer. But Floyd was true to his ambition and remained determined to join the Paras at the bottom.

Four years later, after tough tours of duty in Northern Ireland, Floyd became one of the youngest recruits to the elite of the elite, the Special Air Service. During his time in the military, Floyd has had many adventures and has been awarded the Distinguished Conduct Medal, one of the highest possible awards for bravery – second only to the Victoria Cross. He has also been made a Member of the British Empire. The military story that runs as a thread through the chapters which follow is *not* the story of those events; we do not want to breach confidences or to break trust. But it is a realistic fable of what might happen 'behind enemy lines', and is tailored to illustrate the points we are making in this book.

Whilst in the military Floyd obtained a law degree and later studied psychology. Since leaving the SAS in 2008 with the rank of major, he has been sought after as an adviser to governments, police forces, sports teams and companies large and small. His extremely practical experience of self-motivation and team leadership combines with a detailed understanding of the theories behind it, and it is this special combination that we seek to pass on in this book.

I first met Floyd in the salubrious surroundings of the Lanesborough Hotel at Hyde Park Corner. We come from contrasting backgrounds and have followed very different paths in life. I took to him immediately as an individual. Of course, one has stereotypical expectations on meeting a decorated Special Forces war hero. Floyd fits some of those expectations well – he is tall, muscular, with a steady direct gaze, obviously very strong and fit. But once those hackneyed reactions are over, the main characteristics you notice about Floyd are his aura of extreme calm coupled with a deep reservoir of latent energy. He is easy to imagine as the eye of the storms which so often swirled around him in his military career.

After that first meeting I worried that our personalities were far too diverse for us to be able to work together successfully on this book. After all, I had been one of the boys at school who had always tried to skip games because I disliked getting muddy, cold or hurt. My judgement of Floyd and our different personalities was based entirely on gut feeling, because I had always been sceptical about more scientific approaches to assessing personality. My amateur approach and innate hostility to training, mentoring or advice made me fear that I could not begin to empathise with the book he wanted to write.

My second meeting with Floyd came at the Heathrow Sofitel, where he had just delivered the keynote speech at the annual sales conference of a large gas company, keeping some five hundred delegates spellbound for an hour. There, after his talk, he demonstrated to me scientifically that our personalities were indeed at opposite poles. In the Jungian personality type terminology, which Floyd explains in Chapter Two, he tends towards extroversion, intuition, feeling and perception, and I towards introversion, sensing, thinking and judgement. Then he convinced me that, precisely because his 'ENFP' balanced my 'ISTJ', we could make a great team. He wanted someone, he said, to challenge his thinking and put it to the test. 'You have to have feedback,' he said with a smile, 'Nobody gets to the top of their profession just by being told how good they are. I know you are slightly sceptical, which can only help.' I agreed to do the book. His professionalism had trumped my amateurishness. I had experienced at first hand Floyd Woodrow's motivational skills.

I have spent most of my career as a venture capitalist, investing in early stage technology businesses and helping them to grow. I have sat on the boards of over forty companies. A key part of my job has been to work with the teams running those companies to help them towards their goals. I've been pretty successful in that. Many of the companies that I backed floated on the stock market. Two went pretty much from scratch to being counted among the UK's 250 most valuable quoted companies. Many others were successfully sold. My book *Angels, Dragons and Vultures* is widely regarded as one of the better guides for entrepreneurs to the arcane world of venture capital.

But I am sure that I would have had more success if I had known at the start of my career what I have learnt from Floyd whilst working with him on this book. I now know that if I had taken the trouble to learn more systematically to understand how my mind actually works, how to comprehend my own character, how to recognise other people's personalities, and how to harness that knowledge to achieve my objectives, I could have gone further. You have no excuse, because you now have this book.

This book is relevant for anyone who has ambitions in their chosen field and wants to do well. It should help you understand better how you and other people work. After arming you with that knowledge, it aims to help you to use it to perform better yourself. Based on Floyd's theoretical understanding and practical experience, it will help you to operate better as a member of a team, and as a team leader, and as a team leader of other team leaders. It will equip you with the motivational skills that you need to take your performance to an elite level.

And now a warning: this book is not for anyone who does *not* want to get any better at what they do.

CHAPTER ONE

The magnificent workings of the human brain

You can't make a head and brains out of a brass knob with nothing in it.

Charles Dickens, *Little Dorrit*

'Behind enemy lines'

Floyd leaned forward in the Lanesborough Hotel's comfortable wing chair and rested his elbows on his knees.

'Simon,' he said, 'let me tell you a story about a couple of teams that I have come across in my time in the Army.'

He paused. I waited in the silence of the pause, expectant and rather excited. The intent expression in his eyes held me a captive audience. Floyd cocked his head slightly to one side and I now saw that the intensity was touched with humour, prompted partly by the anticipation he had sparked in me.

'It didn't really happen like this, but it might have. I think this story will show you what I want to get across in the book. I do like the title *Elite!*, by the way, and I will tell you why in a moment.

'I should probably start with a background word or two about the SAS and how it is organised as this is where I really began to learn the skill of leadership. There is no doubt in my mind that we are the best in the world at what we do. We grew out of the group founded by David Stirling in the Western Desert in 1941 during the Second World War to carry out sabotage missions behind Afrika Corps lines. It is said that in the desert war his group accounted for more German aircraft by destroying them on the ground than the RAF managed to shoot down in the sky. The name Special Air Service came a bit later, in 1942. Temporarily disbanded as a full-time unit after the war, the permanent brigade now known as 22 SAS was reformed in 1952. Those of us in 22 SAS generally just refer to it as 'the Regiment'. The Regiment has fought in almost every conflict in which Britain has been involved since the Second World War. We have also been responsible for a myriad of actions that have had a significant impact on world events. The best-known was perhaps the breaking of the siege of the Iranian Embassy in 1981. You must remember that. It was splashed across the media – even live on TV. Men from B Squadron saved nineteen out of twenty hostages, eliminating or capturing six terrorist kidnappers in the process. Most organisations would have seen it as brilliant publicity, but the Regiment doesn't much like being in the limelight. Most of the things we have done have never been made public, and probably never will be.

'Since our formation many individuals have been decorated for bravery. One of those awards, I am proud to say, is mine. But – and this is not false modesty – I would not have that medal were it not for those people around me who performed at a truly elite level. I am just the lucky one who gets to wear it. The same can be said for my MBE.

'Today, there is still the one regular Special Air Services brigade. Nobody is quite sure why it was given the number 22. Someone's lucky number, perhaps. There are also two territorial units, 21 SAS in the south of the country and 23 SAS in the north. The Regiment itself is made up of a number of squadrons. Each squadron is commanded by a major – the rank I attained.

'It is a highly select group; many more apply for the Regiment than pass the extremely demanding and gruelling selection process. What is more, it is the most entrepreneurial business I have ever come across – more entrepreneurial than most of the companies you backed as a venture capitalist, I'll bet. What do

I mean by that? Well, it is constantly looking at ways of staying ahead of the competition. One of the exciting things about being part of the SAS is that you are constantly learning new skills. It is truly elite. And, although I will use the word *elite* throughout my stories, all I actually mean is continually pushing the boundaries of our potential. That is within the reach of all of us and why I like the title of the book.

'Like anywhere in the Services, in the SAS you are expected to obey orders. In action, survival, let alone success, often depends on a rapid, instinctive reaction to what you are told to do. But there is a subtle difference to orders in the SAS. Wherever possible, orders are not narrow and prescriptive. Officers, commissioned and non-commissioned, are encouraged to make sure that their men take responsibility for their own actions, so that insofar as possible how a task is carried out is decided by the man or men doing it. When we plan an action, everyone to be involved in it is expected to make a contribution to that process. Ultimately, the senior officer will take the decision about how it will be done, of course; but all the participants will have had the opportunity to offer input. Even in the field of action, in the heat of battle, we will consult with our comrades if possible. Because we are so well trained to cope with the situations in which we are likely to find ourselves, and have deeply ingrained specialist skills – like some of the parts of the brain that we need to describe in the book – we can make those decisions very rapidly.

'Most people probably have the idea that there is just one type of person in Special Forces units across the world. I bet you had me down as a stereotype before we met. Of course it's true that everyone who attempts to join a Special Forces unit has some common characteristics: you have to be tough, mentally as well as physically; you have to enjoy physical activity, and to relish a challenge, in spades. You have to be able to undertake tasks both as an individual and as a member of a team. But these organisations would not be the formidable fighting forces they are without embracing a diversity of personalities. In any great team, you need different types of people. You need the extroverts, the introverts, the people who analyse the hard facts and those who rely more on their instincts. In the Regiment you will find examples of every personality type.

'I have also been fortunate to be involved in most operational deployments the country has undertaken since I joined the Army in 1981. I can remember each conflict with great clarity, although there are slight differences in my reactions to those events as I became more experienced as a leader.

'The first conflict I can remember was when I was flying back from a three-month training assignment and heard on the radio the news of an aggressor moving their army over the border into the territory of a neighbouring British ally. It immediately sounded like war. Our defence treaty with the country stretched back to goodness knows when. This country was one of our most loyal allies and in a strategically important position. All of this was significant of course, but the most important element of all was that there was a principle at stake. Allow the success of the sort of naked aggression shown by this state, permit the infringement of the rights of a peaceful, independent sovereign state, and the whole world order could begin to totter.'

I found myself nodding vigorously in agreement.

'Obviously at that early stage it was not clear what role I would have in the conflict. What was crystal clear, though, was that I would have a role. The team and I knew we would be assigned the toughest, the most dangerous jobs going. That was what we were there for. What's more, we wanted them.

'Briefings for any deployment pulsate with excitement. But I remember this one better than most. All of us feel some element of trepidation on the eve of a major conflict. But most importantly we look forward to doing what we were trained to do. When I was deployed for that first time on a major conflict, most of us had never taken part in a full-on war.

'I have been fortunate to learn how to operate in the most demanding of environments, whether that was in the bush, in the desert, in the jungle, in Europe or even in the Arctic. But I was particularly excited about fighting in a desert war. I have always been proud of the Regiment's roots in the thin sand of the Western Desert and David Stirling's daring missions behind Afrika Corps lines. And I had heard stirring stories about the key role played by some of our forerunners in the Omani desert in the 1950s.

'I'd passed into the SAS at the first attempt and four years before that I had been in the Paras. The selection course had been every bit as tough as I had expected and I have no doubt that I passed not because I was the finished article but because the people who selected me thought I had some potential. They were willing to give me a chance. I was intensely proud, at the age of twenty-two, to be one of the youngest soldiers ever to make it. In my superstitious moments I thought that my age matching the name 22 SAS could be a lucky sign. Every soldier who joins the Regiment has to start at the bottom, as a trooper, which for many means a step down in rank. Because I was so young, I was only a lance corporal in the Paras.

'Most of the other people I served with were older than me. But in terms of rank I was in the upper half. However, rank matters less in Special Forces than in some other units. The hierarchy is less strict. The key element is that every member is expected to be a leader or a follower depending on the situation. In any arena I was likely to be a follower of others, but if those more senior to me were to fall in battle then I would *de facto* become the leader. Or I might be put in charge of some specific task.

'In the late 80s and early 90s I considered myself highly professional, but, frankly, I was pretty brash and full of myself. I refused to cut any corners at all. I worked exceptionally hard at my training and expected others to do the same. I judged others too quickly and did not listen well. I was not afraid to let people know if I thought they were underperforming. It was not until later in my career that I learned to smooth off some of the sharp corners of my personality and use empathy more effectively. I now know this is critical to effective leadership, and that you have to take into account the characteristics of the individuals with whom you are interacting in order to achieve the optimum result. That's another point I want to get across in our book.'

†

It's all in the brain

Every thought I have, I create. I am in charge of my mind. Probably one of the most important moments in my life was when I realised that everything I do begins with a single thought in my mind and that I control it. Please take a little time to understand this chapter as it is the foundation block of everything you will ever undertake. As I will often say in this book, there is a price to pay to be successful. Understanding how your mind works is part of it.

If you look at your arm, you can get a pretty good idea of how it works. You know what most of the parts are called – elbow, wrist, biceps, triceps, tendons, knuckles and so on. You know that if you tighten your biceps, you raise your forearm at the elbow. You know that if you tense your triceps, your hand will form a fist, and you know why, because you can see the tendons moving in your forearm and on the back of your hand. It may not be simple, but it is clear. It is a comprehensible, mechanical process, cause and effect.

Actually, of course, that is not quite right. In reality, the way you perceive the sequence of events is that you raise your forearm at the elbow and your biceps tighten. You make your hand into a fist and feel your triceps tensing. The effect seems to come before the cause.

Welcome to the workings of the human brain. You think 'I want to pick up that object'. That triggers the act of raising your forearm. You think: 'That person is going to attack me; I'd better defend myself.' That triggers the act of clenching your fist. You don't think: 'I want to raise my forearm, so let's tighten my biceps' or 'I want to clench my fist, so let's tense my triceps.' The unconscious element of the human brain is at work.

Your brain's black box

Most people can name the different parts of their arm. Far fewer can name the different parts of their brain. To many of us, our brain is a black box. It produces a result, creates an effect – of some sort, usually – but we do not necessarily understand why. We may have some vague idea that some people are right-brained and left-handed, or vice versa, and that different parts of the brain perform different functions. But unless we have gone out of our way to learn about the brain, we don't really begin to understand the workings of what most people (apart, perhaps, from certain teenagers) would count as their most important organ.

We also know that if we wish to develop the muscles in our arm we can exercise it, do press-ups and lift weights. After a few days, we can see the physical difference, as the muscles have become larger and more toned. We can also sense the difference because the exercises become easier; after a while we can do more press-ups and lift heavier weights. It is far harder to discern the direct effect of exercising or training the brain.

One reason for this lack of understanding is that we cannot see our brains at work. We can see how our arms work; we can watch those muscles get bigger from exercise. As I said before, it is a complex but comprehensible mechanical process. The brain is closed away in its box. We cannot watch it work.

Another reason is the extraordinary complexity of our brains. And the third reason is that, until relatively recently, scientists were unable to study accurately the workings of the brain. It is only in recent years that rapid advances in medical technology and sensing techniques have made it possible for scientists to understand more thoroughly the functions of different parts of the brain and their complex interactions.

MY HEAD'S A BRAIN BOX AND I NEED TO KNOW WHAT'S INSIDE

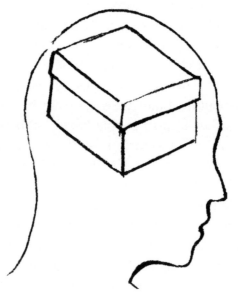

What's going on in my head?

In the course of my career in the Paras and the SAS I have done many, many hours of training. Much of it of course has been physical training, or training in special skills – weapons training, unarmed combat and so on. But I have also spent many hours in leadership training, learning about how to lead groups of soldiers and improve motivation, teamwork and capability to achieve success. Some of those training courses have been immensely valuable, others less useful. But I often felt that there was a missing element, a lack of explanation about what was actually going on inside my mind. I had to learn the practice without the theory because the understanding of the theory was not available at the time. Subsequently, I have had the chance to learn about the theory. The advantage of doing it that way round is that it means you know which parts of the theory really work in practice. This is one of the pillars of this book, which ties together the theory and the practical applications of leadership skills.

Everything we do, every action, every behavioural pattern, starts in our brain. Our brain is our command centre, and it is a command centre that our body cannot disobey. That is why I want to start this book with a brief explanation of how our brains work. I remember once talking to my twelve-year-old daughter about what she was going to do in life. She told me firmly, 'I will make my own decisions about my future, not anyone else.'

'Remember that statement, whatever you do, as you grow older,' I said. 'It is one of the most important things you will ever tell yourself.' It took me until I was in my thirties to understand fully that I am in control of the decisions I make.

My favourite book on this subject is *The Little Book of Big Stuff about the Brain* by Andrew Curran. It is one of those rare books which explain a highly complex subject in a clear and entertaining way. The ability to pull this off always says to me that the author really understands his subject. Andrew Curran draws on a significant body of primary and up-to-date research for his book. I commend it to you if you are interested in delving into this subject at greater depth than I can do here.

In the rest of this chapter I am going to attempt to summarise the aspects of the brain, based on the latest available understanding of it, which are most relevant to our purposes in this book.

There are three main parts to your brain: the reptilian brain, the limbic or paleomammalian brain (both part of your subconscious mind) and the neomammalian brain (part of your conscious mind).

The reptilian brain
The reptilian brain is a fairly basic piece of equipment. It does not care about your children. It does not care about your friends or your comrades. It does not even recognise concepts such as children, friends and family. It sits close to the top of your spinal cord and deals with self-preservation. It makes sure that your heart keeps pumping and your lungs keep breathing, and channels basic

senses like sight and smell. And it carries some very simple selfish reactions. Research on the Mexican green lizard suggests that the reptilian brain is capable of twenty-seven different behaviours: whether to move from the shade into the sun, whether to give way to a larger lizard, whether to grab that ant — all things pretty vital to a lizard's survival. It's important, but as I say, it is a fairly basic piece of equipment.

The paleomammalian brain

As mammals evolved from reptiles about 150 million years ago, our paleomammalian brain began to develop. This is a more sophisticated piece of machinery which began to increase animals' ability to live together in social communities and to nurture their young. With this brain, they started to behave in more complex ways that are not just linked directly to their own survival. These behaviours – nurturing, caring for others, interacting with members of the same species in a social way – are emotion-based. So this is the part of the brain – also known as the limbic brain – which is the seat of your emotions.

The neomammalian brain

Then, a mere four million years ago or so, came the neomammalian brain. This dramatically increased the number and complexity of possible behaviours, and brought the capacity for self-awareness and analysis. This part of the brain is known as the cortex.

To put these different brain mechanisms into context, it is estimated that a human's reptilian brain has fifteen to twenty million nerve cells. Your paleomammalian brain contains perhaps 100 million nerve cells. But in total, the human brain is made up of an astonishing 150 billion brain cells. So the neomammalian brain is around 1,500 times bigger than its more basic predecessors. The number of brain cells you have is one of the things that makes you capable of thousands of different complex behaviours. But, for all of that, wrapped inside your large, recently evolved, rational human brain is that much more primitive emotional early mammalian brain, and, deeper inside still, that very basic selfish reptilian brain. Of course, this layered structure and the way the different layers communicate has important implications for how your brain works and how you can train it. How often are you aware of which part of your brain is operating at any moment? Are you focused on what is actually happening or are you lost in previous behaviour patterns and reacting without thinking?

Wiring your brain

When you are born, most of your brain cells are blank. What is more, they are mostly not really connected with each other. Bit by bit they learn to communicate, building links and connections. Effectively, they wire themselves together. Brain cells do actually grow extraordinarily thin connections from their cell walls towards other cells that are firing at the same time as they are, to form a connection known as a synapse. The synapse is how two brain cells communicate with each other; at the synapse is a microscopically small gap between the cells over which a chemical signal passes.

Brain templates
These patterns of connections in the brain are often known as templates. Once a template is formed, creating a particular thought or action, it can be used again to recreate that thought or action. These recreations are stimulated by memory and may be sparked off by a smell (famously powerful in evoking memories), by a remark or simply by making a movement.

Another word for the formation of templates is *learning*, in the broadest sense. Interestingly, the creation of templates (in other words, learning) in your brain is controlled by the paleomammalian, limbic emotional brain. Chemically, this happens because the substance that is mainly responsible for forming the synapse connections is dopamine, which is released primarily by the limbic – paleomammalian – brain. So templates are essentially formed by emotions, and the stronger the emotion that creates a template, the stronger that memory is likely to be. The stronger a memory, the more easily it can be accessed. Clearly this has important implications for training, teaching and communication.

Teaching your brain

Understanding how to release dopamine effectively is key to good teaching and learning. Stress releases dopamine but in such large quantities that it tends to flood the nerve cells indiscriminately rather than forming the specific synapses necessary to create optimal templates. This helps to explain why memories that are created when you are under stress can be very powerful; a bad or frightening moment in the past, for example, can come back to you repeatedly when it is triggered by a specific word or smell. Over time continuous stress can damage the brain and its ability to learn, and may account for conditions such as post-traumatic stress disorder.

The parts of the brain that deal mainly with memory formation are called the hippocampus and the corpus striatum. The hippocampus handles conscious memory; the corpus striatum deals mainly with unconscious memory. You have a pair of each – one on either side of your brain. The corpus striatum is part of your reptilian brain, while the hippocampus belongs to the more sophisticated world of the limbic brain. Each one is about the size of your thumb.

The amy-what?
Also on either side of your head, just in front of each hippocampus and corpus striatum, sits another, even smaller bit of brain, the amygdala. This is your most basic emotional structure. In primitive creatures the amygdala is primarily responsible for 'fight or flight'

reactions and for sexual arousal. In you it also has a key role to play in the creation of memory. This is how it works.

The two amygdalae sit just in front of your reptilian brain close to the top of your spinal column. They contain receptors for one of the stress hormones, noradrenaline. They are also stimulated directly by the vagus nerve, which connects your brain with your main visceral organs – your heart, lungs, kidneys, intestines and so on. This helps to explain that sinking feeling that you can get in the pit of your stomach when you are nervous or frightened. At times of stress, the visceral organs release adrenaline into the bloodstream, which excites the vagus nerve and stimulates the amygdalae. The two amygdalae in turn flood the two corpora striata and hippocampi with dopamine, creating powerful templates. Memories created like this, at times of great stress, are often your most powerful but can be too intense to be useful.

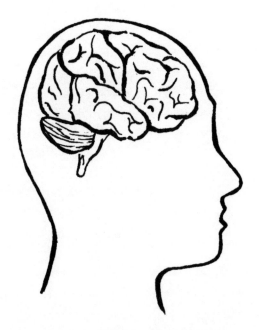

I AM IN CONTROL OF WHAT GOES
ON INSIDE MY HEAD

Conscious and unconscious memory

One interesting feature of memories created like this under conditions of stress is that they tend to reside in your corpus striatum – the unconscious part of your memory – rather than in the more conscious hippocampus. They are therefore difficult to retrieve in a conscious way without real self-awareness.

Dopamine can be released in a much more controlled way through reward and an anticipation of reward. The controlled release of dopamine is how we form the most desirable templates in our brain – or in other words, how we learn most effectively.

New tricks

I once gave a talk to a group of police firearms trainers. A few weeks later I bumped into one of the most senior guys. I remembered that he was one of the people who had sat stony-faced and cross-armed throughout the course. So I was a bit surprised when he came up to me with a broad smile on his face and his arm outstretched. He shook hands with me warmly and patted me on the shoulder.

'Thanks, Floyd,' he said. 'Your talk put me into turmoil.'

I did a bit of a double-take but continued to listen. He saw my surprise and suddenly looked serious.

'You see, I'd always been super hardline in the way I trained – really demanding. I think I really stressed out the guys who came on my course. A couple of days after your talk, my son – he's just eleven – came up to me and said he wanted to enter a golf competition. It was on the tip of my tongue to say "No way" – he'd never even picked up a club before. I thought entering the competition would be a complete and utter waste of time and money. We'd have to buy some clubs, too. It would cost an arm and a leg. Worse, he might do really badly and be humiliated, and put off entering competitions for life. I was about to bark at him, bite his head off and tell him not to be so stupid.'

He paused and drew a deep breath.

'Then I thought about what you'd told us about the importance of emotion in training and the power that using it in the right way could unleash. I looked at Rob – that's my son's name – and I could tell that he wanted to enter the competition really, really badly. I could also see – and this made me feel pretty bad, honestly – that he expected me to say no. It was a really emotional moment. And I said yes. Saying yes would have been worth it just for the expression of surprised delight that crossed his face when I did. We splashed out on some clubs for him, and he practised really hard in the couple of weeks before the contest. He obviously had quite a bit of natural talent for the game, but I reckon it really was the emotion of the moment that inspired him. He learned really effectively and actually went on to win the competition, because he looked forward to the reward of winning that much – and to the reward of thanking me for saying yes. I reckon that moment when I said yes is one of the childhood memories that he will always remember – in a good way. If I'd bitten his head off and said no, it might have been even more powerful but in a bad way.

'But what's more, it did not stop there. When I saw the effect, I completely changed the way I ran my firearms training courses. I dropped my hard line and started using emotion in a more subtle way. I started encouraging them to do well rather than tearing a strip off them when they did badly. The trainees who come on the course probably think that I've had some sort of mid-life crisis and gone soft on them. But why should I care? I reckon it is already paying off in results. I haven't lowered my standards at all – I have just been more effective in getting people to meet those standards.

'Before your talk, I'd have said that there was no way I would change the way I'd done things for years. After all, you can't teach an old dog new tricks. And if there was ever an old dog, it was me. But I guess I was wrong about that, too – the brain is such an amazing thing that if you handle it in the right way it can go on learning whatever age you are, or however set in your ways you are.'

You are never too old to learn

Retaining your ability to learn, whatever your age, however good you think you are at something, is an essential part of achieving elite performance. You cannot remain part of the elite by standing still. You need to remain open to new ideas and new influences and to be willing to adapt. The good news is that your brain can cope with it if you can. However successful a system is, it will eventually become stale and outdated. It will have to be upgraded. The same applies to the files in your brain.

Of course, there are some functions, typically physical functions, which do sit best in your unconscious memory. Certain forms of repetitive training, and of training under a degree of stress, are valuable if you are going to be called upon to repeat those actions without thinking when you are under pressure. That is why Clive Woodward had fire hoses sprayed at Jonny Wilkinson when he was practising his kicking in the run-up to the successful 2003 Rugby World Cup. Really good training can result in knowing what is going to happen before it does. It gives you the ability to act without thinking and to react automatically. Good training follows a simple pattern: learn the skill, put that skill under pressure, then test it. By doing this, the wonderful workings of the brain minimise the stress and the strain when you are called upon to perform it for real. I recently watched an international team perform badly in a major competition. Afterwards I spoke with the leadership team and the players, and we discovered that the team had been practising at 80–90 per cent of their potential during training. They had not been putting themselves under real pressure. The results spoke for themselves. If you want to perform at the highest levels, your training must be of an equivalent nature to what you expect in the arena. The old adage 'train hard, fight easy' always holds true.

Over time you can build up damaging negative files in your subconscious brain. Often these are fear files: fear of failure, fear of conflict, fear of powerlessness, fear of rejection and many others. Later in the book I will describe how to minimise the effects of negative brain files and other limiting behaviours.

I hope that this chapter has given you a bit more understanding of how your brain works, and a few practical tips for how you can make your brain (and other people's!) operate more effectively. However, this is only part of the story because brains are not like Ford Mondeos. Every one is different, unique, even before the start of the fascinating process of forming templates and memories that I have just tried to explain. So my next chapter aims to explain some of the typical differences between brains – the different personality types.

So what?

Remember that you are in control of your brain, not the other way round. Like any other part of your body, you need to understand how it works in order to use it effectively. If you understand how you create the templates in your mind, and the emotions that index those files, you will develop the ability to change them, upgrade them and delete them. To use a filing system effectively, to put data in and get out what you want – especially useful, positive thoughts – you need to know how it is organised.

One of the keys to elite performance is to understand your emotions and how to control and adjust those emotions under pressure. Being in control of the command centre of your actions means that you learn how to diagnose doubt or fear and find ways to adjust your technical skills, tactical awareness, mental toughness and physical abilities. Often we are just told to be more confident, more powerful and more capable without being told how to do it. If you understand how to correctly focus your attention, you will have the best opportunity for elite performance.

Once I realised that I am the one in control of my mind, I began to analyse the files that were helping me and worked out which needed to be upgraded or deleted. I learned that these files exist, even if sometimes beneath my conscious awareness, and that if I wanted to change my behaviour I had to create more powerful files to supersede them and to drive better performance.

CHAPTER TWO

Personality types

Everything that irritates us about others leads us to a greater understanding of ourselves.

Carl Jung

'Behind enemy lines'

'So where was I?' Floyd asked rhetorically. 'Ah yes, as I said before, I am now going to tell you a story, woven together from things I've seen and experienced, about the interactions inside two different teams. The experience of these two teams is drawn not only from my time in the Army but also from my work in the commercial and sporting sectors. As it is my fable, I may even draw on those early days of mine in the SAS.

'It was winter – January – by the time we headed for the RAF base to fly out to another war-torn destination. I was feeling frustrated because it had taken longer for us to take up our role in the conflict than I would have liked. Like the rest of the country, we had all avidly followed the news of the war in the media – the reports of atrocities, the blazing oil wells spewing clouds of black smoke into the sky, the beginning of the relentless pummelling of key enemy targets by the Allied bombers, and the response of artillery launched in defiance towards the surrounding coalition countries. But for all of us it had been frustrating; we wanted to be participants in the events unfolding there, not spectators.

'Nevertheless it was a wrench to leave our families. I had been married for five years by then. I had two children – a four-year-old son and a two-year-old daughter. My wife, Sue, was calm and sanguine – she knew what my job involved – but even so it is tough when we leave our families behind. She had her teaching, and when I was away I could easily picture her daily life. But I knew it would be much harder for her to imagine what I was doing – after all, I did not know myself exactly where I would be and when – and whether I would be in danger at a particular moment. Sue likes facts, although she has an intuitive streak, and she wouldn't have them. I also knew that she tends to keep things to herself so she'd find it hard to share her worries with her friends and family. If I had known then what I know now, I could have described Sue as an INTJ! I also knew that I would have to try to get my life back into balance when I returned, and concentrate on spending some time with my family.

'By then I'd been in the Army for a number of years. I'd worked closely with most of the other soldiers deploying with me and we knew each other pretty well. But we also had a number who had just joined us fresh from selection. As a group we were mostly pretty outgoing, drawing our energy from each other. But there were three or four quiet types who shut themselves away in their private world, even in the transport on the way to the air base. By now I knew better than to try to invade their private space; this was their time, their way of preparing mentally for what lay ahead. The rest of us were chatting, joking and full of excitement, but an element of trepidation sometimes lay behind those smiles. My plan was to relax and get some sleep on the flight. I knew it would be one of the RAF's transport planes, which were reasonably comfortable, and I wanted to arrive as fresh as possible. You never know what will be waiting. We hadn't been told much about where we were going at the other end. It is standard practice not to give out unnecessary information. It might just be useful to people who should not have it and do us damage. You never know. I was always pretty relaxed with that; I felt ready for anything. In broad outline I knew why we were going and what to expect. But I also knew that a couple of the team in their heart of hearts would really have liked to have known a few more of the details. That was just what they were like. So they'd had to get used to the way things were done.

'The flight took about eight hours, I think. With the time difference, we flew through the night and touched down – far too quickly it seemed – at 0800. I didn't get as much sleep as I had hoped. Coming off the plane, the weather was fresh and clear, bracing. It livened me up. The sun was beginning to warm the air after the cold desert night. We piled into covered trucks. The precise destination was still unknown to us, but as we were driving into the sun I could tell that we were heading east.

'It was nearly another eight hours in the trucks so the shadows were lengthening by the time we reached our camp – an airbase somewhere in the eastern corner of the country, ten miles or so from the enemy border. Our lodgings were not the most luxurious, which is hardly unusual – this time it was an aircraft hangar which was already stuffed with boxes of equipment – but I've known a lot worse.

'After a couple of days waiting, the camp can become a frustrating place to be. I filled a lot of my time training and at least we were able to get out of the perimeter to practise our drills. In the military you are constantly training, maintaining fitness levels, and polishing and enhancing basic skills. A key part of the culture is that we are constantly trying to get better at what we can already do well, and learning how to do new things. Before arriving in any conflict area we'd of course learn as much as possible about what to expect. Some of us had been in this environment before. All of us knew not to expect sand dunes everywhere. We knew that the terrain would be much more varied, largely rocky or covered in gravel, in places pretty flat and in others broken up by steep channels. We expected a pretty barren landscape but also a certain amount of scrubby vegetation. It would be dry at this time of the year, but not totally so, as the wadis were often water channels. In places the indigenous population managed to wrest crops of wheat or barley from the ground, and to raise goats and sheep. These desert dwellers were Bedouin, not really specifically belonging to any country, people whose primary allegiance was to their family and their tribe, and for whom a nation was not a natural concept. And we knew at this time of year to expect extremes of temperature – heat in the middle of the day when the sun was up, and cold at night, even below freezing.

'Still, however carefully you prepare for a place, there is no real substitute for being on the ground yourself. So while we waited for action, we took the opportunity to familiarise ourselves with our surroundings and environment, to check over our equipment and to finalise our plans for what we would need to take with us when we were ordered behind enemy lines. For we were sure that at some point we would be given that task.

'There was little real news; we listened to the radio, but I knew enough at first hand about how the Army manages the media and the flow of information in wartime to understand that we were hearing only a small part of the story. From time to time we heard warplanes screaming overhead, especially at night, heading north-east towards enemy cities. I remember that it seemed to me that the frequency of planes increased every night. I guessed that the bombing campaign was steadily intensifying.

'Then at last the call came for us to attend a briefing. We headed for the briefing area in another hangar, which also contained the communication, planning and intelligence functions. The whole place hummed like a hive, buzzing with quiet, focused activity. Our briefing room had no window; it was hot and airless, with no furniture except a few tables laid out in a square in the centre. Some of us sat round the room on the floor with our backs to the walls. A few others perched on the edges of the tables. A couple of the men paced up and down. I pretended to study a large-scale map of the area that was pinned to the wall.

'The intelligence officer in charge of the briefing – an SAS captain – came in. Everyone was immediately alert.

'"You'll be pleased to hear that the time has come for some action," he said. "You can see from the map here that there are two MSRs [main supply routes] running east to west. One of your jobs is to disrupt the activity in those areas. That includes destroying the telephone cables that run in conduits alongside the roads. Our planes have taken out a lot of the comms capability, but the mesh network makes the landlines more resilient and they are still functioning. They've become the enemy's main channel of communication with the missiles that are causing merry hell in the north. You won't have heard it in the media yet, but they bombed a major civilian area last night. It was a bad one and killed a lot of people. Any aircraft found on the ground is a priority target above all others. We believe that the enemy is trying to provoke a retaliation. If they do, it will shake the coalition to its foundations. It is one thing for us to help them sort out a rogue state in their midst, quite another if they find themselves fighting against one of their own alongside their worst enemy. So your second job is to locate planes or missiles and pass any information back to the command centre here."

'He paused to draw breath and looked round the room. He did not need to check that he had our attention.

'"Your zones of operation will be here and here." He indicated two areas perhaps a few hundred kilometres north of our camp. "You need to prepare for a number of weeks' operation there. Over to you to make your plans."'

†

Nature or nurture?

One of the conclusions of Chapter One is that the way your brain is trained – or the way you train your brain – has a big impact on who and what you are. Your identity is so important – how you see yourself and how you like others to see you. The age-old philosophical debate about whether nurture is more important than nature, or vice versa, is outside the scope of this book. But I think that you will agree that nurture – both the effect that you can have on yourself and the effect that others can have on you – is an important element in determining who and what you are. If you ever thought that nature determined everything about you, then you probably made a mistake in buying this book. If you really think that you are born what you are, then you are likely to have a fatalistic view of life and won't have much motivation to get better at what you do. If, after Chapter One, you still think that nature determines everything about who and what you are, then you have definitely made a mistake in buying this book. Elite is something you become, not something that you are with no effort.

Let's accept that part of what you are now is what you were when you were conceived, or when you emerged into the world. A blank sheet of paper is a blank sheet of paper, but the fundamental nature of one blank sheet of paper can be very different from another – rough, smooth, cream, blue. Let's also accept that how you train your mind and your body – what you write on that blank sheet of paper – also has a major effect on what you become.

Everyone's different

Wherever you are inclined to draw the line between nature and nurture, I am sure that you will acknowledge that you are different from me, that I am different from you, and that we are both different from everyone else. You will probably also acknowledge that there are some people who are very different from you, and some people who are quite similar to you. And I think that you may also agree that the ones who are quite similar to you may respond in a similar way to similar behaviour and similar situations.

You may be drawn to some of the ones who appear to have similarities to you. And you may like some of those from whom you seem to be very different. After all, opposites attract, or so they say. You may take an analytical enough approach to your own personality traits to be able to articulate how you will behave in given circumstances, and you may be perceptive enough sometimes to predict how others will behave in those same situations. But wouldn't it be useful to have some tools to help you to understand why you behave as you do, and even more so to help you to understand the superficially peculiar quirks of your fellow men and women; to have an edge in enhancing your strengths and balancing some of your blind spots; to use these skills to communicate more effectively with those who are different from you?

Personality profiling

You may well have carried out personality profiling tests as part of some team-building exercise at work. Depending on your mood at the time, and depending on how well those tests were carried out, and (even more importantly) how well their conclusions were explained, you may have thought that they were a load of old bunkum or that they had removed the scales from your eyes and enabled you to see yourself, your friends and your colleagues in a new light.

And, at the risk of upsetting the sceptics among you, your reaction to the usefulness of those tests had something to do with your own personality profile, and what you are really like yourself. Because there is absolutely no doubt in my mind of the value of personality profiling for understanding and leading yourself, and for understanding and leading those in teams around you. If you read the Introduction to this book, as I hope you did, instead of launching straight into Chapter One, you will know that my co-author started off as a sceptic about personality profiles. I convinced him, and now I plan to convince you.

There are many different types of personality profiling test. The techniques have been adjusted and refined over the years. Some are arguably more suitable for certain purposes, such as recruitment or measuring the likely performance of individuals in a team. In this chapter I am just going to focus on one type, Jungian personality testing.

Jung, Freud and Myers–Briggs

It all started with Carl Jung, the Swiss psychologist who began as a disciple of Sigmund Freud's. Jung published his book *Psychological Types* in 1920 and it sealed his famous split with his teacher. Freud had argued that we are all driven by one fundamental instinct – lust. Had the science of the workings of the brain that I explained in Chapter One been known to Freud, he would have had to construct an argument to say that the amygdala was in absolute control of us. Of course, that scientific knowledge was not available to Freud, so he had to do his best to draw conclusions from his own imperfect observations and suppositions. His theories may have had as much to do with his own sex-obsessed personality and the way that he was himself motivated as with anything else. Jung, also without the benefit of the scientific knowledge that we have now, had the insight to argue that people are different in essential, fundamental ways. He argued that we have many different instincts, or 'archetypes', which drive us from within. These instincts, he claimed, could be of equal importance. The key was each individual's natural inclination to 'extroversion' or 'introversion', coupled with our preference for what he described as 'the four basic psychological functions': 'thinking', 'feeling', 'sensation' and 'intuition'.

At the time, Jung's arguments did not carry the day. His views were more complicated and less sensational than Freud's sex-based theories. So Freud's view of our instinctual drivers became the conventional wisdom explaining our nature, while Ivan Pavlov's theories (he of Pavlov's dogs fame) of the impact of conditioning became the standard explanation for the impact of nurture.

Then, just after the Second World War, Isabel Myers and her mother Katharine Briggs dusted off Jung's *Psychological Types* and created a questionnaire aimed at identifying different personalities. They called their questionnaire the 'Myers–Briggs Type Indicator' (MBTI). Their book of the same name was published in 1962, and it was at that point that the Japanese became interested in their work. Perhaps this interest and their use of these techniques contributed to the rapid growth in Japanese management expertise and economic power through the subsequent two decades. But Myers–Briggs thinking steadily became more mainstream, and by the 1990s over a million people were undertaking the official MBTI questionnaire worldwide every year.

Undertaking a personality type questionnaire

As well as undertaking the official MBTI test, it is now also possible to find many simple, free, self-service personality type questionnaires online (Appendix I lists links to some of these). Especially if you have not done one before, I recommend that you set this interesting tome to one side for a few moments and take the time out to run through one of the questionnaires. It will only take you ten or fifteen minutes.

But before you do break out, it is important to make one point. The purpose of personality profiling is to help to determine your characteristics and preferences. No questionnaire is 100 per cent accurate, and indeed the way in which you answer some of the questions may vary from day to day as your moods change. No questionnaire can substitute for steady observation of another individual over a period of time, and for the application of emotional intelligence. The questionnaire is a tool, a means to an end, not a purpose or an end in itself. It must also follow that no one personality type is better than any other. Extroversion is not better than introversion, or vice versa. It is not what you tend towards that matters but what you do with those tendencies in order to maximise your potential. If the exercise is to have any value, you must answer the questions with this in mind, and avoid the temptation to give the answer that you think (incorrectly) may show you up in the best light. There is no right or wrong or good or bad. I should also add that I was very sceptical about these tests before I completed the questionnaire for the first time.

Now I know better and, as a negotiator, I am sure that this is an invaluable tool when used and practised.

4 x 4 = 16

So you are back!

If you did not know before, you will now know that a Jungian personality type test generates a score between four different tendencies: Extroverted/Introverted (the same jargon coined by Jung), Sensory/Intuitive, Thinking/Feeling (Jung's basic Psychological Types) and Judging/Perceiving (added by Myers and Briggs). You will also know that these combined types are expressed as four letters to give sixteen possible combinations:

ESTP	**ESTJ**
ISTP	**ISTJ**
ESFP	**ESFJ**
ISFP	**ISFJ**
ENFJ	**ENTJ**
INFJ	**INTJ**
ENFP	**ENTP**
INFP	**INTP**

All right, I am sorry, even though I am ENFP, I know that 'Intuitive' does not start with an 'N'. It is not my theory. You will just have to come back to my Yorkshire roots with me and swallow the first syllable. Think of it as 'Ntuitive'.

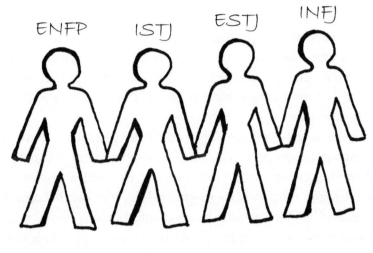

NO-ONE'S A CARDBOARD CUT-OUT

Lost in translation

In fact, I have always thought that a weakness in personality profiling is the jargon used to describe the different types. The words do not really make clear what each means. It may be because Jung wrote his book *Psychological Types* in German and the terms map across to English in an imperfect way. So I am just going to take a little time to explain what each pairing really means. But before doing so, I will repeat my earlier word of caution: the questionnaire is a guide and it does not know you better than you know yourself. If you have scored heavily on one characteristic but believe you fit more with another, trust yourself. However, do not make the mistake of thinking that you should score higher or lower in a particular category just because you like to think of yourself more or less that way.

Scales

You will also know from scoring your own test that each of these characteristics appears as a range or as a scale. It is possible to be right at either end of the scale, or somewhere in the middle.

And it is important to factor this into your understanding of the results. Depending on where you are on the scale, you may have a very strong preference for a certain type of behaviour, or you may be quite closely balanced. It is also important to remember that you are still unique even though you sit in one of the sixteen categories. You are just similar to those in the same category.

There is a temptation to think that you have all of these characteristics in perfect balance. So, when a careful analysis is required, you can bring your 'Sensing' element into play; when the situation demands more gut feeling, you can become more 'iNtuitive'. When a hard-headed approach is right, you can magically become 'Thinking'; when a softer approach is needed, you can move across the scale to 'Feeling'. Certainly, when I first did these tests I was arrogant enough to believe I combined all of the elements equally. I know now that this was a naïve attitude, and that I do have a preference for one side, even though slight, in certain areas. Being a particular personality mix, whether it is ENFP or ISTJ or whatever, is also not an excuse for behaving in a particular way. The purpose is to show where you are strong and where you may have blind spots or filters.

Now the jargon

Extroverted/Introverted is actually about energy and where you get it from. Extroverts get their energy from interacting with people and activities, whereas introverts focus on their inner world of ideas and experiences and get their energy from within.

Sensory/iNtuitive is less clear because you can interpret the two words in similar ways. But what Myers and Briggs meant by 'Sensory' is being observant of the real individual physical things around you, and aware of the details that make up a picture. And by 'iNtuitive', they meant imaginative, more focused on the big picture and its overall abstract or theoretical meaning.

Thinking/Feeling is clearer again. By 'Thinking', they meant tough-minded, tending towards being objective or impersonal with others. 'Feeling' implies more softness and being sympathetic or personal with others.

Judging/Perceiving is slightly confusing again. 'Judging' means making and keeping schedules, whereas 'Perceiving' means being more open to options and alternatives, and more willing to go with the flow.

It is also important to understand how each group tends to like to be presented with information.

Sixteen possible personality type combinations

There is not enough room in this book to explore in detail all the sixteen possible personality type combinations. The original 1962 book, *The Myers–Briggs Type Indicator*, is out of print, but if you are interested in delving more deeply into this fascinating subject the closest alternative is *Gifts Differing – Understanding Personality Types* by Isabel Briggs-Myers and her son, Peter Myers. Or you could try *Please Understand Me* by David Keirsey, which some people see as the standard modern work on this subject. Keirsey gives names to different letter combinations, so SPs are Artisans, SJs Guardians, NFs Idealists and NTs Rationals. According to Keirsey, an ENFP (my category) is a 'Champion', and an ISTJ (my co-author Simon's category) is an 'Inspector'. My personal hesitation about Keirsey's book is that he expresses a strong personal preference for Artisans as a character type, which threatens to undermine the impartiality of the process. As soon as one starts making value judgements suggesting that one type is somehow 'better' than another, one can prejudice the whole process because people will tend to want to be categorised as that type.

It's a difficult choice, but my personal preference for further reading on this subject is *Leadership and Development* by Lee and Norma Barr.

Testing your friends

I hope that doing the questionnaire earlier helped you to understand the make-up of your own personality. I doubt it did more than confirm what you already knew instinctively, but it may have provoked the occasional wry smile as it confirmed a particularly strong trait that your friends have told you about in the past.

Of course, you cannot get every person that you meet to complete a personality type questionnaire before you start interacting with them. However, I do have some favourite questions that I might sometimes ask to clarify in my own mind the characteristics that someone tends towards. So if you ask someone whether they can happily stay alone in a silent room for a long time, the 'E' will give a metaphorical shudder and say, 'No – it would be like a prison.' The 'I' will shrug their shoulders nonchalantly and say, 'Yes – for quite a while; I quite like being by myself.' Showing someone a complicated photograph and asking them what they see will result in the 'S' (the 'Sensory' type) describing to you in some detail the objects in the picture; the 'N' (incorrectly for 'iNtuitive', remember) will attempt to explain the concept behind it and make sense of the picture. If you ask how someone likes to be rewarded for successfully completing a task, the 'T' will tend to want a tangible reward such as promotion or money, whereas the 'F' is more likely to say that a simple 'thank you' or a pat on the back is sufficient. Telling someone that they have a notional deadline to deliver a report and asking whether they will hand it over well in advance or on the final date will sort out the 'Js' (early finisher) from the 'Ps' (at the deadline).

Putting up the shutters
All this can be important because if you present information to a particular personality type in the wrong way, the shutters can come down and your message may not get through because of the filters people build deep in their minds. Remember the brain in Chapter

One. Once you build files in your mind they can be lost deep inside and play without you being aware of them. So if you need to get something done, it will probably not be a problem to set a deadline for someone with a 'Judging' personality, but to get the best result out of their opposite, the 'Perceiving' type, may require a different approach. Often you need to be careful about your choice of words and use of language; a 'Sensory' individual is likely to respond best to a clear and accurate factual approach, whereas an 'iNtuitive' individual may require more of a conceptual story.

Body language

The body language of the individual with whom you are communicating is an important feedback loop. If they are really engaged, they will be making eye contact, nodding, perhaps holding their chin in their hands in a thoughtful pose. If you are not getting through, their arms or legs may be crossed and their eyes may be avoiding yours. You may need to remind yourself consciously of their personality type and adapt your way of communicating.

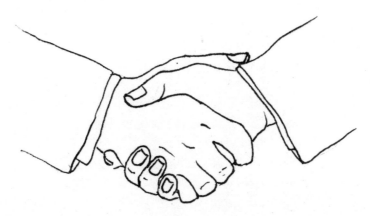

GET A GRIP ON YOUR BODY LANGUAGE

Another important part of the vocabulary of body language is mirroring. Mirroring an individual's behaviour – sitting in a similar position, using similar speech patterns – is a powerful way to win their rapport. Observing whether their body language mirrors yours or not is a good way of testing how much rapport they have with you. Of course, mirroring negative body language is likely to have the opposite effect of reinforcing the barriers between you and the person with whom you are trying to communicate.

There is more on body language in Chapter Four, which is about negotiation and communication.

A hostage to fortune

It was 0400 hours one morning in December. The phone rang. It was the CEO of Britam, the security company of which I became a director when I left the SAS.

'Floyd – I'm sorry to wake you, but there's been a kidnapping in Afghanistan. A 24-year-old woman who works for Acme plc. She was out there travelling to Kabul from Pakistan with just an interpreter. There is no sign of him either. They found the car on the outskirts of Kabul. That is all we know. And I am afraid there are some bloodstains on the back seat. No ransom demand has come in yet, but Acme need someone to get them ready for the negotiations that are likely to follow. Can you do it?'

I was wide awake by now. My mind started to churn through the normal sequence of events in these cases. 'Sure. How soon do they want me? Where are they located?'

'Their corporate HQ is over in London. Their team will be gathered there by 0800 hours.'

It is rare that the make-up of personalities in any team is the perfect mix. As I have already explained, one of the main benefits of understanding our personalities is so that we can all adapt our styles if we want to when necessary. However, as the lead in this particular situation, I had to enhance and accelerate our communication, so understanding the people I was about to work with as fast as possible was going to be essential.

'Can you get the profiles of everyone in the team sent across to me? And any other background information that you think will help me gain rapport quickly with them – family, hobbies and achievements. Also some background on the company. I also need all the information about the woman, her family and the interpreter.'

I settled automatically into the three-hour drive, and concentrated on mulling over the situation. It was time to build a game plan and visualise how this was likely to proceed. It was also time to think about a contingency plan. I've heard 'visualisation' talked about quite often without a clear explanation of why it is necessary. The mind's filing system does not differentiate between what you actually see and how you see something in your imagination. I visualise in two ways. First by imagining that I am looking as an observer at the event in which I am going to be involved. That morning, I imagined meeting with three or four people and how our initial meeting was likely to go. Second, I imagined the event as if I was seeing it through my own eyes and watching what was happening. The additional critical element in this second approach was that I connected emotionally with the visualisation. I imagined how the people in this case would be feeling, how I would feel, how the people who had been kidnapped would be feeling. This gave the visualisation substance and meant I was better prepared when I walked into the pressure zone. I could also practise the event as many times as I liked; the practice was free! How often do you actually practise in your mind what a meeting will entail, how a conversation or presentation will actually go?

I got into London a bit early. The overnight security guard was still on the reception desk and he directed me to the boardroom. I was there first, so I started to scan the information I now had on the company and key directors and to develop further the game plan we would need. Then a knock came on the door and a secretary led me to the CEO's office. I found three worried people there – the CEO and his number two, and the Group Director of Human Resources. Their polite smiles of greeting faded fast. Their handshakes were clammy. The reality of the situation now dawned on them. One saving grace I knew from the due diligence we had done on the company was that this team had practised this situation with another negotiator. So at least they had been through the theory behind a situation like this. If I am teaching a company how to prepare, I run through a lifelike simulation with them. I build a picture of the situation and play newsreel footage that I have made to replicate the type of media response that is likely to follow such an event. I use Twitter and Facebook feeds to complicate the situation by criticising the response of the company and blaming the CEO. I use media and journalists to ambush the team and ask for an instant response, and video the interactions of the team to replay what actually happened during the exercise. This is done to put the team under pressure and enable them to learn how to adapt to a complex and difficult situation. I hoped they had had a similar programme.

'Thanks for coming, Floyd.' The CEO looked as if he had had a sleepless night but was still brisk and businesslike. 'We haven't got many of the facts yet, so it is hard to make an accurate assessment of the situation.'

'We do need as many details as possible, I agree, but the important thing is that we get her back safely.'

'It certainly seems important that we get on with it,' the CEO's number two chipped in. 'We can't wait until we know exactly what has happened – we need to get on to think about the possibilities. And it seems to me that we need to be really careful about how we communicate with the kidnappers. Clarity of language is going to be important.'

I spent the next hour with them in deep discussion. The CEO was logical, analytical and objectively critical, as well as being decisive and assertive. The HR director was practical, realistic and tended to be optimistic. He had the warm and tactful style that you would associate with a good personnel professional. The CEO's deputy was a highly capable woman and seemed a good foil for her boss – more interested in theories and concepts, but capable of objective analysis and of asking good questions in an assertive way. Watching how they spoke and interacted, I made the following assessment.

We had possibly got ESTJ, ESFP and ENTP personality types. With me as an ENFP fronting the negotiation, I reckoned it was not a bad negotiating team, but it could be strengthened considerably by someone who was more inwardly focused and who would help to integrate ideas in a systematic, logical way – an INTJ, for example.

We were evenly balanced between sensing and intuition, but, because the CEO tended towards sensing, that would give an edge to this way of absorbing information. The group would respond well to starting with facts and detail, but I would check that they did not lose sight of the overall picture. We were also evenly balanced between 'Thinking' and 'Feeling', but the edge here went to the 'Thinking' group, again because the CEO was one. So I would need to ensure they were aware of the more emotional elements required in this situation (for example, how we communicated with the families, workforce and media). And finally there was a balance between 'Judging' and 'Perceiving', but the group was once again likely to go the CEO's way and would want order and a resolution as early as possible. I knew that this was not how these situations often play out and that I would need to keep the group aware that we would not be able to follow a precise plan and would have to adapt accordingly. The crucial point was to understand that people are different. They make decisions and have biases that may be different from the way I make decisions and my own biases. Understanding personality types gives me a tool to adjust my communication style and connect with those around me. We now defined our roles and responsibilities and made sure people stayed aligned with the overall strategy throughout. I placed the names of both hostages up on a board so that everyone could see that they were the key people in this. We had the correct people in place to make sure that debate was robust; we could be objective and ensure that our decisions were based on proper analysis of the facts. We learnt from our decisions and adapted them when necessary.

The initial conversation with the hostage-taker made it clear that he had done this before and simply saw it as a business negotiation (although I use this term, it is still extortion, and one must never lose sight of the danger in these situations). This was good news for us as it meant that he wanted to find a practical solution. He also spoke English so we did not have to work through an intermediary. He understood the process and expected to go through a series of discussions with us before defining a price for the hostage. He had all of the answers to our questions very quickly. Proof of life was quickly established. He even ensured that one of the questions we asked was clarified because he did not think we were being clear and he did not want to risk delay by allowing us to misinterpret the hostage's answer. It became obvious that the hostage-taker was an extroverted type because he talked his ideas through openly, even speaking over the CEO on a number of occasions, and avoided silences. He wanted finite detail of the plans to drop off the money. He was very flexible and it did not seem to matter too much if we had to change plans or timings. He spoke of the woman and his concerns for her well-being and her family. But he also indicated that he was prepared to hurt her if required in order to force our discussions to a conclusion. At least his threats were initially about depriving her of comforts rather than immediate physical injury.

Our reaction to risk was so important now that we needed robust debate; we needed to anticipate all possible contingencies and create different creative solutions where necessary. We also had to learn to adapt our decision-making time from hours in some cases to minutes in others. During this process I became a leader or follower depending on where my strengths lay. Because I understand myself, I also know when I am about to become stressed. It was important that I use my own strategy to rebalance if it occurred. For myself, I know I have to think logically, then factually and then emotionally. I am also aware of when others become stressed and I attempt to rebalance them. I ensured that the team stayed focused on the end result and did not lose sight of what we wanted to achieve in the first place. We also ensured that we understood the environment in which we were working and kept the stakeholders alongside and dealt with any implications the situation had for this team from a business perspective. The team gelled very quickly. They were able to listen to different perspectives, give their views and move forward. Even in tough times when unexpected things happened, such as the involvement of the military and police, the team stayed calm and relied on one another to come up with solutions to deal with them.

The hostage-taker had taken a deeper interest in his hostage than one might perhaps have expected. Because he was so talkative it became easier to get more intelligence from him. As we built an element of rapport we were able to establish that he had a family of his own and I was able to link the hostage's needs to her own family. I managed to get him to use her name and the interpreter's name so that he would begin to see them as individuals. I had him marked down as an ENFP and this understanding made it easier to handle him as effectively as possible.

Absorbing data

I will discuss in more detail the interaction of different personality types in teams in Chapter Five. For the time being, I want to end this chapter with a summary of how individuals of each type like to absorb data. This is important to understanding both how you interact with the outside world and how you can best interact with others. If you imagine that someone is selling something to you, and you find yourself warming to the proposition, it may be because the product or service is good and something you want. It may also have something to do with how the information about that product or service is being presented to you. The two initials which are most relevant for how we take in data are the middle two, the 'Sensory/iNtuitive' and 'Thinking/Feeling' pairs. Table 1 summarises the negotiation or sales approach that is most likely to appeal to different personality combinations.

Table 1. Relating negotiating styles with personality combinations

STs will want to be shown:	SFs will want to be shown:
• that the product works • how it saves time and money • that it has a good cost-to-benefit ratio • how its results can be measured • all its other applications and benefits	• the product's practical results for *people* • its benefits for themselves and those they care about • that it provides immediate results • explicit, not just implicit, benefits
STs will want all their questions answered, and will like to try the product before they buy.	SFs will like a presentation that shows them respect and sets the product in a personal context. They will be influenced by personal testimonies from other users.

NTs will want to be shown:	NFs will want to be shown:
• details of the product's research base • its theoretical background • how it fits a specific strategy • how it will increase competency	• how the product will enhance relationships • how it will help people develop • how it will give new insights • why people will like it
NTs will want information presented in a credible, factual way that supports the product's far-reaching possibilities.	NFs will like a presentation that focuses on people's unique gifts, shows that the product will help them find meaning, and is enjoyable and fun.

So we've dealt with the workings of the brain in Chapter One. Now we've discussed the theory of different personality types. In the pages that follow I will refer back to what I have covered in these first two chapters to try to draw out some practical lessons.

So what?

You may think that you have a good understanding of your personality and the impact that you have on others. However, a systematic approach to analysing your own personality will take your self-awareness on to the next level. You will gain better control over your behaviour and the effect it has on those around you.

Applying the same principles to those around you and gaining a structured appreciation of their different personality types will give you a clearer idea of how best to relate to others. Your ability to communicate will improve and you will be better able to manage any situation to achieve your objectives.

I use these tools at home with my family, in all my social relationships and most of all when I am working. Whenever I start working with a new group, I take them through a personality assessment. It instantly opens up better communication with the group. It allows me to ensure that I adapt my communication style when necessary to get my message across without misunderstanding. How often have you heard two people arguing with each other yet saying exactly the same thing? Understanding how you come across, and how your counterparty wants to hear things, are the two essential elements to delivering your message.

CHAPTER THREE

The North Star: understanding your own priorities, aims and objectives

Adversity is the first path to truth.

Lord Byron

'Behind enemy lines'

Floyd paused again. 'I've been talking too much.'

'Not at all,' I said. 'Don't stop. We are just getting to the exciting bit.'

Floyd grinned. 'Maybe. But we are certainly getting to the "fabulous" bit. Remember I said at the beginning that my story was not going to be true. Now I've bamboozled you by giving you a lot of realistic background. That's what all good storytellers do. But now I am going to undermine my good work by reminding you that this is a fable, a fiction designed to illustrate the themes of our book. You've probably spotted a few of those already – my references to different personality types, the importance of training, and so on. But now you will see that it really is a fable, because I am going to be in two places at once. I am going to tell you about both of the groups that go behind enemy lines.'

'I knew you SAS guys could do anything, even to the point of defying the laws of time and space.'

Floyd ignored my bad joke and ploughed on.

'So the group was divided into two groups of eight. Let's call them Delta Eight and Delta Nine. Splitting teams like that for patrols is pretty normal practice. In command of one was a staff sergeant. Let's call him Martin; in the Regiment we almost always use first names, not ranks. Martin was a seasoned soldier in his second decade in the Army. He had his team's profound respect, and they felt good having him in charge. As number two there was a corporal, Tom. Three of the others in the group – Steve, Wings and Kevin – knew the staff sergeant and the corporal well; they'd worked together on several occasions. Three had passed selection and joined in the months running up to the conflict, so they were less well-known quantities, but that success alone demanded respect. Two were ex-Paras – Mick and Colin – and one – Geordie – came from the Marines. Geordie's real name was Steve, but he came from Newcastle, and Martin had started calling him Geordie to avoid confusion with the other Steve. The name stuck.

'They were all good soldiers. They'd trained hard together and the seasoned guys had made a conscious effort to get to know the new ones and make them feel they belonged to the group. What is more, Martin had put his entire team through a personality assessment. You might not think that we do that sort of thing in the Army, but we are often ahead of the game! David Stirling himself was something of an expert in identifying the correct type of people he needed around him.

'They looked round the room at each other. The expressions of mutual respect and trust were just as they should have been. Their lives would depend on each other and without absolute mutual faith their security would be at still greater risk.

'"So," said Martin, "it's clear to me that we'll need to take vehicles. We are going to have to take a lot of equipment, food for three weeks, water. There'll be way too much to carry on foot. We know what it is like carrying that amount of stuff from the practices we've done. It's just too hard."

'Colin, one of the newer guys, piped up. "Couldn't we get a plane to drop us off – or parachute in? We'd get to our ops zone quicker, and with less risk of detection. We could stash our heavier gear; just take what we needed day by day. We could easily fit that into our rucksacks. And with no vehicles we'd need no fuel, which'll take up half the space on its own."

'Tom – the corporal – shook his head. "I don't like the idea of stashing our kit. There is too much risk of it being discovered, and then we really would be up the creek. We'd also be tied down to one place and keep having to go back. Too much risk of ambush. We've got to keep everything with us and make sure that we are totally mobile at all times."

'"Yes – and with vehicles we can get out of there quick if we are spotted."

'"But just having the vehicles raises the chance of being spotted. I'm not sure that there is much scope to conceal anything as big as a Land Rover in that terrain."

'"We'll find somewhere, I'm sure. Some of the ground is flat, sure – pretty good for driving, in fact – but there are plenty of gullies and dry riverbeds. And away from the MSRs themselves the desert is pretty empty."

'"That's why…"

'"… it's called desert, dumbhead. Yeah, I know." Grins broke out round the group and some of the tension ebbed from the air. Only one guy hadn't spoken.

'The staff sergeant drew him into the discussion. "Mick, you're very quiet – what do you reckon, then?" Geordie tried to cut in before Mick could speak.

'"Hang on a moment, Geordie. It's Mick's turn."

'Mick grinned and continued, "I reckon it has probably got to be vehicles. We do need the speed and mobility – and the load-carrying capacity. No two ways about it."

'Heads nodded. Martin looked round the room. "Is each of you happy with the plan? Are you ready to commit to it?" An affirmative chorus greeted his question. "Colin, are you okay with that?"

'Colin grinned. "I know that you are all just scared of low-level night flying. You didn't all have the benefit of my time in the Paras. But yes, it makes sense. I'm with you."

'So the plan was settled and they turned their attention to digging out their equipment. To carry eight men and equipment you need two vehicles. We use long-wheelbase Land Rovers, which are pretty good in this environment. They are known as Pinkies because they are painted a sandy shade of pink. Long experience has shown that this is the most inconspicuous colour in desert conditions. They also carry camouflage netting. The Pinkies were mounted with twin Bren guns – general-purpose machine guns – which would have the advantage of dramatically increasing the patrol's fire power. It was true that diesel – and water – made up a large part of their load, but there was also plenty of room for their personal weaponry – automatic rifles with ten spare magazines of thirty rounds each, grenades and portable machine guns.

'They spent a morning at the range zeroing the rifles and checking the magazines, practising the basics yet again. Other vital equipment was plastic explosives with timers for destroying the telecommunication ducts along the MSR. If they did encounter any missile launchers, the plan was to call down an air strike rather than attempt to destroy them from the ground, and each Land Rover carried a long-range radio for this purpose. You could only use them sparingly because their signal could easily be picked up by enemy direction-finding equipment and could give away the patrol's position. For communicating between the vehicles in case they got separated, or if a group broke off from the vehicles to patrol on foot, they had two short-range radios that operated on such a low wattage that they would be almost impossible to detect. The communications equipment was completed by four short-range line-of-sight radios, which could also act as emergency beacons or for communicating with planes overhead. Delta Eight planned only to use these if something went wrong because their signal was also easy for the enemy to detect.

'Everyone knew that they operated best if they were well fed and rested, so they stocked up with plenty of energy-rich rations and took lightweight but warm sleeping bags. The plan was to be on the move most of the time during the cold of the desert night, but the winter weather is unpredictable and one cannot be too careful. Unnecessary discomfort always reduces energy levels and effectiveness. Then, of course, they took medical supplies in addition to the first aid material each soldier carries in his belt kit, including the two Syrettes of morphine that standard operating procedure demands each man should carry around his neck.

'When everything was ready, checked and double-checked, the patrol relaxed a little and waited to be told when they were going in. The word soon came that they would move out after dark, so the afternoon was occupied with formal orders. This is a standard procedure where, in addition to all the members of the patrol itself, everybody else involved in the operation gathers. The patrol commander ran through the whole plan from start to finish, telling everyone what they already knew to make sure they really knew it. An up-to-date report on local conditions was provided by the intelligence officer – expected weather patterns and data about enemy movements, for example. Then, finally, the orders in written form – each sheet overprinted with the words"Remember Need to Know"– were handed over to the operations centre so that there was a clear record of the plan, of where they expected to be and how they expected to get out, in case anything went wrong. This is known as the E&E plan.

'After the order briefing, the members of Delta Eight had a little time to sort out their personal things in case they needed to be sent back to their next of kin. Then, as dusk began to fall, they piled into the Land Rovers and set off north towards the border. They aimed to get there just as night really fell so that they could make as much ground as possible towards their destination during the hours of darkness.'

†

Careers consultancy

When I was thirteen I went to see the school careers consultant. I knew exactly what I wanted to do. I was going to join the Paras when I left school, aged eighteen or sooner if I could manage it. Then, at the earliest possible opportunity, I would join the SAS. When you are thirteen, ten years seems a lifetime, so after ten years in the Army I planned to become a PE teacher. What's more, I knew exactly why I had mapped out this career path. The Paras and the SAS would be more challenging, more physically demanding, than anything else I could do. The PE teacher bit – well, in all honesty that was way over the horizon, although I always had a desire to teach sport.

I explained all this to the careers consultant. He wore those half-moon glasses and somehow managed to look over the top of them and down his nose at me at the same time. 'Woodrow,' he sneered, 'with your grades and lack of application, you have about as much chance of getting into the Parachute Regiment as the Devil has of Heaven.'

This, of course, is one of those early memories that were seared into my brain in the emotional way I discussed in Chapter One. The careers consultant could have given me this feedback – which, in all honesty, was correct – in a much better way. But I don't think he was trying to motivate me or stiffen my spine; he was just unskilled in communication and delivering feedback. Maybe I do him a disservice and he read me like a book and pressed exactly the right buttons. Because whatever his intentions, it certainly did make me more determined than ever. I trained hard over the following years, and by the time I reached eighteen those fearsome physical tests for the Paras, although a challenge for me, had become passable. The rest, as they say, is history. I joined the Paras aged eighteen and then the SAS at twenty-two. I never became a PE teacher, but I had married one by the time I was twenty-four, so I always felt I was ahead of my markers!

A sense of vocation

In many ways I think it makes life easier if you know with absolute clarity what you are aiming for, like I did. I did not spend any time worrying about whether I should do this or that; I just focused single-mindedly on achieving what I had decided to do. That sort of approach also has its drawbacks, of course, and I appreciate that most people do not have a vocation in the way that I did. But I do think it is important to ask yourself at the start of your career what you can achieve, and to keep asking that question periodically as you move through life. At many important stages in life there is a clear choice. As Morpheus puts it to Neo in the film *The Matrix*, 'You take the blue pill, the story ends, you wake up in your bed and believe whatever you want to believe. You take the red pill, you stay in Wonderland, and I show you how deep the rabbit hole goes.' *The Matrix* wouldn't be much of a movie if Neo had chosen the blue pill. And if you like the taste of the blue pill, you probably shouldn't be reading this book.

As I neared the end of my Army career it was rather different. I did not have absolute clarity about the next step in my career. To help me decide what I was going to do next, I tried to accumulate as many new skills as well as I could. I studied law and psychology, and learnt how to fly. I realised that of these alternatives I was most interested in psychology. So a role in coaching, training and motivation became my next goal in life. I often speak to young people who are unsure what career path they should tread. I always tell them to do as well as they can in their studies and take as many jobs and roles as they can; they will eventually find the correct path for themselves.

A race into the pressure zone

There is a school called Christ College in Brecon, in the same mountainous national park where I used to do a lot of my training. It is a great school, excelling academically and at sport. One of their sports is cross-country running – partly because the demanding geographic location is great for training – and they've spawned quite a few national and international champions. One day I went there to watch a race. The Welsh weather was typically cold and wet and there was a strong wind blowing, driving the rain almost parallel to the ground. The junior team was aged between eleven and fourteen; the senior team ranged from fifteen to eighteen years of age. This race was a vital event for the senior team because they needed to win to progress to the next round of the competition. Because it was a team event, they had to have a full complement of runners to win. Each runner's scores counted and all runners had to finish the race. The trouble was, one of the senior team was missing.

The headteacher turned to the junior team with a pretty grim expression on his face. I knew he did not want to put the next question; he was worrying that it was asking too much.

'Will any of you juniors volunteer to run in the senior team? It will be really tough – you'll have to run fifteen kilometres instead of the five kilometres you are used to. I won't blame you if you decide to stick with the junior race. But …' His voice trailed off.

The silence deepened. Feet shuffled. I looked away. After about twenty seconds, the smallest child stepped forward – she was a young girl who looked about eleven – and said, 'I'll do it.'

That day she ran three times farther than she had ever run before; she was sick three times whilst running around the course; she was sick again after she finished. She did not win, but she did not come last either. Christ College gained enough points to go through to the next round of the competition. Without the girl they would not have made it.

I spoke with the girl after the race. She was still sweating and red-faced from exertion. I was bursting with admiration for her.

'Well done, that was amazing. But why did you do it? What made you step up and volunteer?'

She had to take a big gulp of air before she could answer. 'I just wanted to push myself. I wanted to see how good I could be. I now know how good I am. And after today, I now know what to do about it.'

Let's just analyse her statement.

The North Star vision

'I just wanted to push myself. I wanted to see how good I could be.'
That is her vision, an unambiguous statement of intent, something so clear that you can describe it in a few seconds. I love to hear a vision in which I can see that its holder truly believes, because I too can feel what the success of the vision would mean. It blazes above the horizon like the North Star so that you can see it no matter what the adversity, high enough even in the fog of battle. I can't tell you how many times I have been told by people that I could not achieve something, only to prove them wrong in the end. I almost take it as a point of reference because once people doubt I can achieve something, I know I have set the bar at the correct height. How many people in your own team or organisation actually know their purpose? Without clarity of direction, how do you prioritise work, how do you keep focused in adversity? How do you know when you have got there?

YOUR NORTH STAR VISION:
CLEAR, UNAMBIGUOUS AND VISIBLE
NO MATTER WHAT THE ADVERSITY

The starting point

'I now know how good I am.' This is her start point. Understanding this is so important. Where am I now? How good am I at this moment? You must be able to look in the mirror and be honest with yourself. Being honest is fundamental in evolving and upgrading your capabilities – your *technical skill*, your *tactical application* in the marketplace, your *mental toughness*, your *health* and the culture you operate in. Being technically good, tactically aware, mentally tough and physically capable are key elements and the foundation of elite performance. With them in place you can adapt to any situation. But it is also important to make a regular and honest assessment of the start point. When you can do this effectively, you become your own coach – and a very effective one, too.

THE START POINT ALLOWS YOU TO
UNDERSTAND HOW GOOD YOU ARE TODAY

Stepping into the pressure zone

'I now know what to do about it.' This I call 'stepping into the pressure zone', the arena where you need to perform at your best. Understanding the pressure zone and getting used to being in it are crucial. Once you step into the pressure zone, and understand

how to make appropriate decisions, driven by fact, adaptability and creativity, you begin to perform at the highest levels. The more you challenge yourself, step into this zone and practise there, the better you become at dealing with pressure. When I talk to groups of any type I often bring an empty chair to the front of the room. I tell the audience that I am going to select someone to sit there and that I am going to place them under enormous pressure. Then I pause. The room always goes silent. The only noise is inside the audience's head as their inner voices come to life, repeating the words 'please do not pick me'. This is because they do not want to fail in front of the others. However, the more you can see this situation as an opportunity, the more used you become to pressure, the better you will be able to deal it.

THRIVE UNDER PRESSURE

Commitment

Then you must make the commitment to improving and stepping towards your purpose and vision. I see too many people who have all of the talent in place yet fail to commit and take that step forward. One of the wonderful things about the human brain is that once you believe and commit, it uses its huge power to find ways for you to achieve what you want. Self-motivation is an essential part of commitment. It is rare that you will achieve anything without this component.

Aoccdrnig to rscheearch at Cmabrigde Uinervtisy, it deosn't mttaer in waht oredr the ltteers in a wrod are, the olny iprmoatnt tihng is taht the frist and lsat ltteer are in the rghit pclae. The rset can be a total mses and you can sitll raed it wouthit a porbelm. Tihs is bcuseae the huamn mnid deos not raed ervey lteter by istlef, but the wrod as a wlohe.

In other words, once you know the ending and the beginning, you can fill in the gaps; your mind will find the links.

REACHING YOUR DREAM TAKES
COMMITMENT

Nothing is impossible

I've always had a fundamental belief that I could achieve anything if I really wanted to, not because I am naturally talented but because I am prepared to keep trying and learning in order to do so. So what I've always done is put myself in different environments to see if that is true. If you asked me whether I honestly believe I can do anything that I want to do, then I'd have to give you the answer 'Yes.' That answer and that belief have been developed and enhanced by all the people I have worked with and the great things I have seen achieved. I am constantly inspired by people of all ages who attempt to push their boundaries and get that little bit better and closer to their goal. Again, commitment is key. I see too many talented people who could tackle complex problems, but they do not believe in themselves and do not commit. Without commitment, nothing happens.

It is critical for anyone aspiring to take their talent to the limit to ask two key questions. The first question is: 'Am I really hungry to achieve what I want or am I prepared to settle for second-best?' And the second question is: 'Am I willing to pay a price for my success?' Because there is always a price to pay.

But a bigger price tag hangs off second-best. On that price tag it says 'time'. Time is a truly priceless commodity because it cannot be bought or sold. It cannot be given away or saved up. In an eighty-year life span one has just 4,160 weeks, or 25,565 days, or 613,560 hours. You might have more; you might have less. No one knows. But I do know that it is too valuable to spend settling for second-best.

The 'F' word

I often ask my audiences to name their greatest fear. Whether the audience is made up of eight-year-old children or Special Forces soldiers, or any combination in between, they come up with the

'F' word, the worst 'F' word of all: 'failure'. The brain templates that form when you experience failure are especially powerful, with the result that you can remember your moments of 'failure' with painful clarity. The mind can replay to perfection the events and feelings connected to a 'failure' and also interlinks to all the other times you have 'failed'. I will explain later some of the techniques to help minimise the effect of these feelings.

For me, the word *failure* only exists if I give up. Otherwise it is an inhibitor to performance. It is far too laden with value judgements, too black and white, too final. If you think of the possibility of failure before you start, the fear of failure may prevent you starting. That is probably what was at the back of the other children's minds in that junior running team at Christ College. I often see adults who are afraid to step into the pressure zone because of the fear of failure and the debilitating effect it can have on performance.

I have reframed the word *failure* for as long as I can remember. Instead of using that 'F' word, I use the word *opportunity*, because every event is an opportunity to learn and do better when you try again. How on earth can you expect to learn without making mistakes? The answer when you do make a mistake is to dust yourself down, get up and start again.

I love this extract from Theodore Roosevelt's famous 'Citizenship in a Republic' speech at the Sorbonne in Paris in 1910:

> It is not the critic that counts: not the man who points out how the strong man stumbles or where the doer of deeds could have done better. The credit belongs to the man who is actually in the arena, whose face is marred by dust and sweat and blood, who strives valiantly, who errs and comes up short again and again, because there is no effort without error or shortcoming, but who knows the great enthusiasms, the great devotions, who spends himself for a worthy cause; who, at the best, knows, in the end, the triumph of high achievement and who, at the worst, if he fails, at least he fails whilst daring

greatly, so that his place shall never be with those cold and timid souls who knew neither victory nor defeat.

Optimism

People of my personality type – ENFP, in case you have forgotten – tend to be quite optimistic. We are not given to a great deal of self-analysis. We don't spend a lot of time agonising about decisions or revisiting ones we have made. So, once I decided it was going to be the Paras and the SAS, I did not spend any time worrying about whether I had taken the wrong decision. Sure, there were some difficult and uncomfortable times. If I had allowed myself to think about it, there were even some moments when I might have preferred to be doing something else completely different. But my training, the way my brain and body had been exercised over the years, helped me to focus on the task in hand.

These iNtuitive, Feeling, Perceiving characteristics perhaps make it easier to find a vocation and to stick to it. Replace any of those with Sensing, Thinking and Judging, and you are more likely to want to question and analyse the life choices you have made. So I fully understand that some of you reading this book may find my single-mindedness alien. My rather simple way of motivating myself and setting my priorities and objectives is not necessarily the best way, or the right way. Some of those close to me might even have said at some points, when my relentless focus appeared to exclude what they needed, that it was the wrong way. As I said in Chapter Two, no one personality type is 'better' than any other. None of us have a monopoly on the right way of looking at the world.

There are some useful techniques which might help you to work out your motivation and ambitions. They don't work for everyone all of the time, but personally I have found them helpful when from time to time I have needed to rebalance my life and decide my priorities.

The Wheel of Life

The first technique is known as the Wheel of Life. It is an approach that helps you to balance your use of time and to understand where to focus your energies. It works like this.

Draw ten circles inside each other. Then label each circle from 1 to 10 from the middle outwards. Now draw eight spokes so that it looks like a wheel. Then think about the things that matter most to you in life – you might like to list, in no particular order, 'career', 'family', 'friends', 'money', 'love life', 'nutrition', 'fitness', 'security', 'environment', 'leisure activities' (perhaps subdivided for specific hobbies). Label each spoke with one of these items. If you have more than eight items, add another spoke to the wheel. You should end up with something looking like Figure 1.

Figure 1. The Wheel of Life template

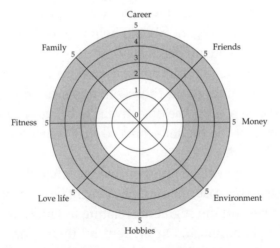

Now give each segment a score out of ten for the current level of your satisfaction with that aspect of your life. Join up the points on each spoke and you will have a picture like Figure 2.

Figure 2. Your complete Wheel of Life

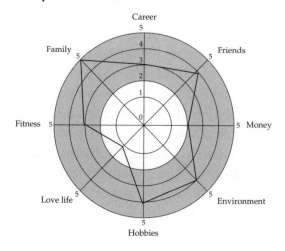

This may not tell you anything that you do not already know in your heart of hearts, but it will give you a quick visual picture of the balance in your life, and should help you to clarify if there are areas with which you are dissatisfied.

Clearly, to achieve optimum satisfaction, you need to focus your efforts and energy on those segments to which you have given the lowest scores. The objective is to bring the lower scores up to the level of the higher scores so that your Wheel of Life is perfectly balanced.

Of course, there will be times in your life when the wheel is out of alignment. In my case, for example, I might be away on a mission for six months, and the segments relating to family, relationships and friends will diminish. On my return I then endeavour to get the wheel back towards balance by focusing on the parts of my life that I have been forced to neglect.

The Two Chairs

Another technique that I use I call the 'Two Chairs'. If you will excuse the pun, it can stop you falling between two stools.

Put two upright chairs opposite each other. Sit down on one. Imagine another 'you' sitting in the chair opposite. This is 'you' in five years' time. Visualise yourself in the perfect way, after all the things that you want to happen. What do you see? Picture yourself. You are older, of course; you cannot do anything about that. You may be greyer, but I want you to imagine yourself looking fitter, in good health, wearing clothes that you like, feeling happy about who you are. I want you to imagine the house you are living in, the car you are driving, your ideal family situation. I want you to think about the dreams you have and imagine that the person opposite you has attained them. Imagine all the things that you have done for your personal development, your hobbies, the financial targets you have achieved. I want you to imagine all your relationships with family and friends being successful. I want you to look at the achievements in your work. Remember to visualise yourself in the best possible way.

When you are totally happy with the person you picture in that empty chair, stand up. Go and sit on the empty chair. Now imagine that you are the successful person who has achieved everything that you have just thought about. Imagine the thoughts and feelings you would have. Now look back at the chair that you have just vacated. Imagine telling the old you what you have to do over the next five years to get from where you are today to where you want to be in five years' time.

Once you have an understanding of your vision you can start to make plans for how to achieve it. Personally, I look to build a support system around me as I prepare to see through the fog of events that will occur along the way. To lock my goal in my mind, I find a picture of something that provides a symbol for my vision. I then reinforce my objective by placing that picture where I can see it every day.

All of this is simple, common-sense stuff, I know, but it can be surprisingly helpful in really focusing your mind on what you need to do to achieve what you want.

IT'S NOW TIME FOR THE FUTURE
YOU TO TELL YOU
HOW TO GET THERE

Sticking to your guns

Whatever your mindset, whether you like a lot of data to help you or whether you prefer to rely more on your gut feeling, you need to reach a decision and stick to it. If you do not take a decision, you will never be able to make a commitment. If you are on a journey and you constantly change your destination, you will never enjoy the satisfaction of getting to the end. You will be wandering aimlessly and ultimately be dissatisfied. Often it may not be possible to work out what your ultimate destination should be. You may have to take your journey one stretch at a time. By all means divide your journey into manageable lengths. You may find that when you have completed one leg of your journey, you head off on the next one in a direction that you might not have originally predicted, with very positive results. But for each phase of the journey, you must take a decision and make the commitment.

It is unlikely that you will have absolutely everything you want to take a decision, whether it is based primarily on 'Sensing' or on 'Feeling'. If you have two-thirds, or three-quarters, of what you want to take a decision, you are doing pretty well. Life is ambiguous and there is often no single right or wrong answer. What really matters is taking the decision. Whatever your personality type, putting the decision behind you, removing the uncertainty, can be a cleansing process. The act of taking a firm decision is the first step on the road to success.

Remember that you cannot win by playing safe. If you choose the blue pill over the red, you will be consigning yourself to mediocrity. You will never be elite. To be elite, you have to take risks. You have to seize opportunities. You have to challenge yourself. You have to step into the pressure zone.

If that sounds daunting, it's because it is. Rising to a challenge is … a challenge. But the more you prepare yourself for that challenge, the less daunting it becomes, and the greater your chances of success. Remember that *failure* is not a word I use, so the choice is not between success and failure. The choice is about making the opportunity as successful as possible. To do that, you need to communicate well. You need to be able to negotiate your way through the maze. You must be well prepared, well trained. That is what the next two chapters are about.

So what?

At times in your life you may have clear goals and objectives. At other times, it may be harder to see the way forward. Some of the techniques outlined in this chapter may be helpful in identifying your goals. If at the start point you cannot see very far forward, break your journey into discrete, identifiable milestones. But above all, take a decision, and commit to achieving that goal. Don't let a fear of failure prevent you from taking advantage of an opportunity, because it is only by stepping into the pressure zone, by stretching and challenging yourself, that you will move towards the satisfaction of elite performance.

Once you get used to being in the pressure zone, it becomes exhilarating and you want to be there more often. You get used to testing yourself and extending your capabilities. Tennis genius John McEnroe always said that he lived for the pressure points because that's where it counts. It is easy to make a good shot when there is no pressure, but it is far less satisfying.

CHAPTER FOUR

Communication and negotiation

Courage is what it takes to stand up and speak; courage is also
what it takes to sit down and listen.

Winston Churchill

'Behind enemy lines'

'So what about Delta Nine then?' I asked.

'Delta Nine, yes. What about them?' Floyd raised his
eyes towards the elegant mouldings on the ceiling of the
Lanesborough's tearoom, and thought for a moment.

'In my fable, Delta Nine decided to do things slightly
differently. Or perhaps I should say that they decided differently
to do things. Like Delta Eight, they broke out after the briefing
to make their plans. They were a slightly unfortunate mix of
characters, brought together from various other groups. Four of
them were pretty loud, including the sergeant (the highest rank)
and the corporal. These four were very close, too, really good
mates. It was interesting, because this inner group included two
of the newer guys – Billy and Chico. I think these two really
looked up to the corporal and the sergeant, who seemed to enjoy
the admiration, so they bonded unusually quickly. The other four
tended in the opposite direction and were pretty quiet. Strangely
enough, this quiet bunch included the three most experienced
soldiers in the group.'

'So I'm guessing that their planning session went a little
differently.'

'You could say that again.' Floyd grinned. 'Actually, one of the new guys – Billy – chipped in first in an eager tone: "So how do we get to the ops zone, Jim? You've done this sort of thing plenty of times before. What's the best way in your view?"

'The sergeant puffed his chest out a bit. "It's a three-way choice. Either we take a couple of Pinkies and drive up there, or we get ourselves dropped off on foot by plane, or we parachute in. It's a straight choice."

'"Well, we're not exactly going to walk three hundred bloody miles carrying all our kit, are we?" This comment was muttered *sotto voce* at the far end of the room, and the sergeant did not quite hear what was said. The two guys sitting on either side of the mutterer – Stu, one of the longer-serving troopers – did though, and twitched slightly.

'The corporal raised a brief laugh – from half the group, anyway – with his next comment. "Give me the choice of a short ride in a plane and a long dusty drive and I'll go for the ride any time. The terrain out there is pretty flat; if we do take the Pinkies, I don't see how we can hope to keep them out of sight."

'"That's probably right, Stan," agreed the sergeant. "The trouble is we will have a lot of weight to carry, especially at the beginning, when we have got our water."

'"We can hack it, Jim," said Billy eagerly. "We are all big and strong enough. God knows we've humped big enough packs on training. What's all the training for if we are not going to do it for real?"

'"Let's work through what we will need," said the sergeant. "If we are going in on foot, we will have to keep our kit down to the minimum. Stan, why don't you make a list of the essentials? Weapons, ammo, explosives. We can keep the weight down by not taking too much comms stuff – one long-range radio to call in the strike if we find any missiles or planes should do it. We can't avoid one five-gallon jerry can of water each – that'll be forty pounds on its own, but at least it will get lighter as we drink it. Fourteen days' worth of rations, of course, but that won't take too much space.

Forget things that are too bulky, especially heavy clothing. I can't believe it will be that cold at night in the desert."

'"We'll be moving around at night, anyway. It'll be a piece of cake!"This comment from Chico, one of the new boys, attracted a grunt from the quiet group of four at the other end of the room but no dissension.

'This time Jim made an effort to engage the quieter members of his group."You guys have all been pretty quiet. Are you okay with the plan?"

'Stu looked up and briefly met the sergeant's gaze."Sure, we're okay with it."The others shuffled their feet uncomfortably but did not say anything.

'"Good, that's sorted then. Let's get on with gathering the kit."

'Three of the eight men had still not spoken.

'The rest of Delta Nine's preparations followed a similar pattern to Delta Eight's. They did their time meticulously on the range, preparing and checking the weapons. Their A-frames were packed with great care, spreading equipment and supplies between them, so that if one of them was lost, for whatever reason, the consequences would not be too dire. They too went through the order briefing and sorted out their personal possessions. Then, a few hours after Delta Eight had headed north in their Land Rovers, they were driven out to the landing ground to board their plane.

'In spite of Stan's comment about preferring a ride in a plane to a long drive, they aren't exactly the most luxurious form of transport going. They have no seats for a start, just a bare hull, and you have to make yourself as comfortable as you can on the non-slip floor. They stink of aviation fuel, and the heat from the engines makes them unpleasantly hot even in cool weather. The flight to the drop-off point was a little over an hour and did not pass uneventfully.

'They flew low level to avoid being spotted. As the plane contoured along the terrain several of the soldiers were violently sick. They were given a fifteen-minute warning and began to fix on their equipment. When the RAF jump-master called them forward they checked each other's gear. The jump-master then did a double check. The side doors of the aircraft slid open and the sudden rush of air and noise focused everyone's attention. They all shuffled forward, almost bent in half by the weight of the heavy equipment strapped to their chests. Then came the two-minute warning, the red light and the green, and they were all in the air. The remaining heavy equipment was hurled out behind them. They made a good landing close together. They knew that this was the moment when they were at their most exposed and vulnerable. Four members of the patrol lay in all-round defence covering the whole 360-degree arc with their weapons, while the remaining members of the team hurried to gather their mountain of heavy equipment.

'With some dismay they noted that their landing location was very open – not what they had expected from the maps they had studied.

'"Bloody hell, Jim. Are we in the right effing place?"This was Stan, the patrol's corporal, addressing the sergeant. "I thought there was meant to be some cover round here. It's as flat as a pancake. Shouldn't we head back and reassess where we are?"

'"It's too late to turn back now, for God's sake. Just get the kit together so we can move off as quickly as possible."

'"Stan may have a point, you know, Jim. What if we can't find a good LUP anywhere close?"This was Billy, one of the new guys. LUP's short for Lying Up Point, by the way.

'"Just shut up and get on with it. We'll find somewhere. What sort of pussycat are you? We'll discuss our next steps when we've found our LUP."

'"Right."Satisfied that their landing had not been observed but keyed up, Jim snapped into action."Stan, you stay here and guard the cache with Billy, Stu and Evan. Come with me, the rest of you, to recce for a good LUP. The map showed that there should have been some high ground and cover right here, but it looks as if we are going to have to cast our net wider. Expect us to be back within the hour."

'In the event, Stan and his three comrades had a much longer wait. It was a good three hours before the recce team returned. The night air of the desert was much colder than they had expected, and a chill had worked its way into the cache team's bones. "I wish we'd brought some warm kit," Billy muttered to Stan. "This is real brass-monkey weather."

'"It wasn't my idea to leave that gear behind, mate."

'The news from the recce team wasn't great either. Jim seemed in a foul mood. "The first bit of broken ground is a good three Ks north of here. We have found a dry water channel up there that'll give us some cover. It's not the ideal LUP, but it'll have to do. I reckon we've been dropped off further south than we should've been. We really need to get a move on if we are to shift all the kit up there before dawn."

'Delta Nine had a back-breaking night. The only practical way of moving the equipment was in relays. With their weapons, radios, explosives and water, they must have had nearly three-quarters of a tonne of kit between them – a good eighty kilos apiece. However strong and fit you are (and there was nothing wrong with Delta Nine's strength and fitness), you cannot carry that sort of load non-stop. So while they each kept their A-frames on all the time, and their belt kit of course – you never take off your belt kit – weighing about thirty kilos combined, they had to take it in turns in two groups of four to carry the rest of the stuff. They did manage to get to the LUP and stash all the equipment before first light, but only just.

'Billy and Stu got the first stretch of stag – sentry duty. As they made their way to the higher ground overlooking the dry watercourse that was to be their base for the day, Billy muttered to Stu, only half in jest, "I knew I shouldn't have complained about the drop-off point." Stu grunted, taciturn as usual.

'Meanwhile, before settling down to try to get some sleep on the hard desert ground, Stan and Jim were having a conversation of their own.

'"Jim, I really do reckon we've made a mistake. We should have come in vehicles. We have far too much kit to carry and our mobility is going to be compromised. In this open ground we're too easy to spot and if we are spotted we will not last long. I'd vote for returning to base and reassessing the situation. Then we can redeploy."

'"That is a big call, Stan," replied Jim. "Admitting failure this early on goes against the grain. Think about it. We'll talk about what to do later." Stan shrugged.

'Their council of war took place towards the end of the afternoon. The day had been pleasantly warm after the cold night but now, as the shadows lengthened and the sun was touching the western horizon, the temperature was dropping fast. An ominous bank of cloud was gathering to the north, and the wind appeared to be freshening.

'Stu was back on sentry duty. "He never has anything to say anyway," joked Billy. This brought a couple of smiles from the others, but those faded fast when they heard what Jim had to say.

'"Stan and I reckon we were dropped twenty Ks further south than intended. That means to get to our area of operation we are going to have to move all our equipment forward again to where we should be or split the group with one team remaining here and the other team going forward to recce the ops area. Then we can reassess the situation."

'He paused and looked around the group. Several of the team stared down in dismay. Billy kicked at the ground. Chico, one of the other younger guys, broke the silence. "How did we get into this mess?" Stan was next. "Well, it was either us or the pilots who effed up. But there's no point arguing about it now. I've thought about it and as far as I am concerned it's too early to admit defeat. All we can do is soldier on." Another pause followed and then Jim spoke decisively. "Right, here's what we are going to do. You four will remain here. You three will come forward with me and recce the area. When we get back we'll make a decision."

'A rock rattled across the ground and everyone looked up. "What do you mean, here's what we are going to do? Don't you think it would be better if we discussed the options properly this time and then made our decision?"

'Jim glared at Gus, the youngest member of the troop, in an unguarded, instinctive reaction."What do you think we have just been doing? And what do you know about it? You have only just joined us. Does anybody else want to say anything? No? Fine – Billy, Chico, Stu, you'll move forward to recce with me. Be ready to move out at last light in thirty minutes. The rest of you will stay here."'

†

Communication is negotiation is communication

In Chapter One I tried to provide some insights into the workings of the human brain. Chapter Two covered one aspect of the brain's different manifestations, in the sense of the various personality types to which it can give rise. Chapter Three focused on motivation, and the objectives you set for yourself in your brain.

This fourth chapter is about communication, and about negotiation. It is not possible to write about negotiation without writing about communication, or vice versa, because virtually every time you communicate you are negotiating too. And every single time you are negotiating you are communicating. This chapter pulls on some of the threads of the preceding chapters; you need to understand something about people's personal characteristics and their preferences in order to be able to communicate with them effectively, and you need to understand your own motivation and objectives to give your negotiation any point and purpose. This chapter also looks forward to what comes later in this book – to working in a team, and leading a team and teams of teams. That is because communication, and the negotiation that accompanies it, are vital skills whatever your team role.

Simple communication or subtle negotiation?

Consider the simplest forms of everyday communication. When does a statement or a question become a negotiation or the start of a negotiation? *'I am going to watch* The X Factor *at 7.30 tonight'* at one level is a simple statement of intent. But it is also potentially the opening gambit in a negotiation. Even if the answer is, *'Fine, that's a good idea; I'll watch it with you'*, there may have been an undercurrent of unspoken negotiation: *'You know I hate that programme but I cannot be bothered to argue about it right now ...'* If the answer is, *'I'd much prefer going out to see a movie; why don't we do that instead?'*, then an explicit negotiation has begun. If the invitation to spend the evening in the delightful company of Simon Cowell goes unchallenged, and no explicit negotiation takes place at that moment, the event may nevertheless be stored away for future use: *'I watched* The X Factor *with you last week, so now it's fair for you to come to the movies with me.'*

Even a simple offer to do something has an element of negotiation about it. *'I am going to get myself a coffee. Would you like one too?'* may sound like a totally altruistic offer of a hot beverage, but in fact it probably carries the expectation of a future *quid pro quo*. *'Would you like me to get you a coffee?'* may be essentially the same offer, but, because it does not carry the implication that I am doing it for myself so it is easy for me to do it for you too, its *quid pro quo* expectation may be firmer.

I am not advocating turning every domestic conversation into a negotiation to which you should apply the techniques I will outline in this chapter. If you did, you would soon become very wearing to live with. Anyone who has brought up children through their teenage years knows how tiring an endless negotiation can be: *'Yes, if you are back by 11 tonight you can go out late on Saturday ... No, not midnight, 11 ... No, if you are back after 11, you will have to stay in on Saturday; it is school tomorrow ... All right, if 11.15 is when the bus gets in, then I suppose that's all right ...'* and so on.

But I am making the point that there is a process of give and take, an expectation that if I do this for you, you'll do that for me, hard-wired into the human psyche. The clearest-cut negotiations may take place when you are trying to agree a price or terms of a deal with a buyer or seller, or to obtain better economic conditions for yourself or your company in a certain situation. And tenser negotiations involving hostages or military situations of the sort in which I have often been involved may be more vital in terms of life or death. But the principles that apply to all are very similar. And communicating and negotiating effectively are an essential part of being elite. My understanding of the different personality types of my children and family members has been invaluable in communicating with them.

A good definition of negotiation is 'a conversation with a purpose'. And just what's the point of a conversation without a purpose?

Preparation

The first rule of successful negotiation, as of so many things in life, is careful preparation. Before I go into a negotiation, I make sure that I know the answers to the following questions, in order of priority:

- What *must* I have?
- What would I like?
- What do I know about my opponent?
- What is my plan for the negotiation?

What *must* I have?

The 'must have' from a negotiation is known by many different names: the line in the sand, the bottom line, the deal-breaker. In certain circumstances it is clear, cut and dried: if you are talking a suicidal person down from a tall building, the 'must have' is no jump. If you are arguing for the release of hostages, the 'must have' is that they should be freed unhurt. But in most commercial circumstances, it is less clear. At what point does a price or a contractual term really become unacceptable? Is the 'must have' a single item, or a blend of variables? If you go into a negotiation without clarity about what you must have, you will end up in a muddle because you risk losing sight of why you are negotiating in the first place. You come back to your vision or purpose and must articulate a clear statement of intent.

What would I like?

Then there will normally be a range of secondary options, or 'nice to haves'. If the 'must haves' are your unshakeable strategic goals and set the firm framework for your negotiation, the 'nice to haves' will inform your negotiating tactics. Winning as many 'nice to haves' in a negotiation, without prejudicing your 'must haves', is one of the things that can make bargaining fun. Clearly ranking your 'nice to haves' – *I'd rather pay 10 per cent less than get two extra for free* or *I'd rather sell twenty and be paid a month later than fifteen and get cash up front* – before you start negotiating will enable you to be much more decisive and to react more effectively in the course of the discussion.

What do I know about my opponent?

Sometimes you find yourself negotiating with someone you know very well – that recalcitrant teenager, or the partner who prefers to stay at home and watch *The X Factor*, for example. On many occasions in the wider world, however, you may have to negotiate with someone the first time you come face to face with them. However, that does not mean that you have to enter the battle unprepared. In certain circumstances – the hostage-taker, for example – an army of researchers may access secret files to prepare a dossier on an opponent. But in most normal situations, background research is easier and quicker now than it has ever been, thanks to the power of the internet. There is little excuse not to carry out a quick Google search on an individual you are about to meet, and on the organisation they represent. Indeed, it is almost impolite in our era of easily accessible information not to have checked out a person's background before a meeting; it almost implies that you do not care. I was recently involved in a counter-terrorist training exercise. I asked how much they had found out on the internet about the athletes who had been captured. The look of horror that crossed their faces at the realisation that they had not accessed this simple information was indeed interesting.

It is also worth remembering, by the way, how much your own on-line profile can give away. Some on-line data is hard to change, but consider what your entries on social media platforms such as Facebook, Twitter and LinkedIn might say to people with whom you might one day be in negotiation.

If the meeting is an important one, it could well be worth probing a bit deeper. Is there anyone you know who has dealt before with the individual you are about to meet? If the meeting is in order to discuss a deal or a sale, is there anything useful you can identify about how they might behave, about their negotiating style or their likes and dislikes?

If you cannot find any way of checking out your adversary before the negotiation meeting, then picking up signs and gleaning data quickly when you do meet become doubly important. Clearly, you are not going to be able to get your opposition to complete a personality test before you start (unless, perhaps, you are recruiting them, in which case a personality profiling exercise can be useful in telling you how to hire them as well as telling you if you want them or not). But in the small talk that starts most meetings, you should be able to learn something about your counterpart's personality in the way I suggest in Chapter Two. Does their reaction to the view through the window suggest a Sensing or an iNtuitive approach? Does their demeanour hint at an Extrovert or an Introvert style? Sometimes in meetings people chat for a while and then say, 'Now let's get down to business', or words to that effect. Actually, of course, that time spent exchanging niceties is very much part of the 'business', and gives the smart negotiator the opportunity to adjust their communication plan to fit more closely to size. If you are in your counterparty's office, a quick look around at pictures, photographs, awards or framed certificates should provide useful information about what is important to them. How things are organised and laid out, whether it is tidy or chaotic, may provide other clues.

Two words of warning:

1. Don't allow your prejudices to infect your approach: *'He's an ex-soldier, so he'll be tough'*, or *'He's young, so he'll be inexperienced.'* Stereotypes are just as often wrong as right.
2. Remember that your opposite number may well be checking you out in just the same way. The first impressions that you make really count. Make sure that the first impression you give is the first impression you want to give.

What is my plan for the negotiation?

'I have a cunning plan' was Baldrick's catchphrase in the hilarious television series *Blackadder*. His 'cunning' plans always landed his master and himself in trouble. But there is no question about it; it is far better to enter a negotiation with a clear plan than without. The plan should start with your own opening position, but it should also be mapped out several moves ahead, like any good chess player would. *If they respond like this, our next move is that. But if they ask for this, then we offer that.* And so on.

Obviously it is not possible to plan for every eventuality, but it is a good rule of thumb that the more important a negotiation, the more meticulous the preparation and contingency planning should be. A useful exercise can be to do a role play, with a colleague playing the part of the person with whom you are about to negotiate. In these role-playing exercises, I also put people under pressure by shouting at them or being objectionable in some way or other. Once they get over the shock, they realise that if they do interact with someone like this they are already prepared. This indeed was the case when I worked on a very large negotiation involving numerous parties each out for their own gain in total disregard for one another's position. I prepared the team that was trying to bring each of these groups together by putting them through an intensive negotiation mimicking the people they were going against. When they came back they smiled and said it went exactly as we had planned. They had had to stop themselves from smiling when someone blew up and tried to take control of the meeting. I am also involved in numerous interviews for high-profile jobs. It still staggers me how ill-prepared some senior people can be in interviews.

One of the great benefits of having a negotiating plan is that it can give the impression of spontaneity. If you have worked things out beforehand, instead of thinking about a response to a gambit, and giving the impression of being cautious and guarded, you can come straight out with your answer, appearing open, direct and confident. I often say that my most spontaneous moments were planned months in advance.

Negotiation style: win–lose or win–win?

Part of the planning process for a negotiation is to think through what style of outcome you want. In some circumstances, the only acceptable outcome may be a win–lose. For example, the concessions sought by the hostage-taker for releasing his captives may just be impossible to meet, and there may be an absolutely irreconcilable conflict between his 'must haves' and yours. You may have to push him to a position where he loses, and does not get any of his 'must haves', and where you win by getting the hostages released safely.

But in most negotiations you do have a choice about how far you push your opponent, and the style in which you do it. The transaction you are discussing may be a one-off, and you may therefore not care too much about whether you leave your opponent feeling bruised and battered. So if you are buying a house, for example, squeezing the price as hard as possible may be the right approach because you are very unlikely ever to have to deal with the same vendor again and getting that few thousand extra off the price can really make a big difference to you.

However, in most commercial negotiations there is a probability that you will want to deal with the same individual again. Repeat business is often the best business. Even if a particular transaction seems to be a one-off, news about negotiating style and reputation can spread. Bruise an opponent too much in one negotiation, leaving them smarting, and it may rebound on you. It may be that they are acquainted with a person you meet in the next transaction. Or they may reappear in another guise later in your career. You do not want to gain a reputation as someone who is unreasonably hard to deal with, because there is normally someone else offering an alternative to what you have. If you leave too many bruised egos in your negotiating wake, you may find that fewer and fewer people wish to do business with you, and that those who still do fight your negotiating style with heightened intransigence of their own. There is a lot of truth in the old adage 'What goes around, comes around'.

So, in most normal circumstances, the ideal outcome of a negotiation is where both parties feel that they have fairly achieved a satisfactory result. Both sides need to have won in the sense of achieving their 'must haves', and to have each chalked up a few of their 'nice-to-haves', which, of course, may not be in direct conflict with each other. One side's 'nice-to-have' may well be the other side's 'happy-to-give'.

To me, effective negotiation involves achieving your goals in a manner that maintains and enhances your relationship with your opposite number. To do this, you need to empathise and build emotional links with the person on the other side of the table.

Firm but fair is the right negotiating reputation to build.

Active listening in building rapport

The different steps in negotiation were systematised by the Federal Bureau of Investigation in the 'Behavioural Change Stairway Model'. This model – BCSM, for short – was developed by the FBI Crisis Negotiation Unit in response to emergency and hostage negotiation incidents. The BCSM depicts a method of progressing from a position of crisis through distinct, linked negotiation phases in order to achieve behavioural change such as the surrender of the perpetrator or the suicidal individual. At face value, the FBI's BCSM is simple, but it has proved extremely effective in the operational arena.

The original model had five key stages:

1. Active listening
2. Empathy
3. Rapport building
4. Influence
5. Behavioural change

As you can see, 'Active listening' was the original first step up the stairway. However, in training it was observed that student after student initially used active listening, but that, as the process moved forward, they forgot this crucial element – with negative results. So the model was adjusted as shown in Figure 3.

Figure 3. Revised Behavioural Change Stairway Model

		Active listening
1.	Empathy	
2.	Rapport building	
3.	Influence	
4.	Behavioural change	

Listening actively to your counterparty is the most important element in any negotiation. If the negotiation gets stuck you can quickly utilise your active listening skills to move things forward again or at least to buy time in which to replan.

The specific stages in the BCSM cannot be rushed. You have to empathise first and use this as the base for building rapport. It is easier to influence someone once that rapport has been built and they have realised that you have, in a non-judgemental way, taken the time to listen to them and to see things from their point of view.

Although the BCSM was developed for crisis negotiations, the principles and the steps – the need to move through the four phases whilst listening actively all the time – hold good in any type of negotiation.

Emotional intelligence

Research demonstrates that high intelligence or verbosity are not qualities that make good communicators and strong negotiators. Instead, excellence in communication and negotiation is associated with intelligence of a different kind: emotional intelligence.

Coupled with its cousin, active listening, emotional intelligence is the key characteristic that the negotiator requires to move his opponent up the BCSM. In particular, the negotiator needs to be able to read his own emotions and recognise their impact on his opponent. He has to control his emotions and impulses in order to make sure that they are not damaging but produce the right effect. He then needs the ability to sense, understand and react to his opponent's emotions and to influence them while managing conflict.

Excellent communicators are able to note small tell-tale signs both in the way their own emotions are affecting the other party and in the emotions being expressed, sometimes accidently, by the other party. In psychological jargon, these are known as 'somatic markers' which can form the basis for an instinctive reaction or a 'hunch' about someone.

As Peter Drucker put it in his book *Management Challenges for the 21st Century*, 'The most important thing in communication is to hear what isn't being said.' For more on the importance of emotional intelligence, try his book or Daniel Goleman's *Working with Emotional Intelligence*.

STEP INTO EACH OTHER'S SHOES

Empathy

Emotional intelligence is the key characteristic you require to develop empathy with your negotiating counterparty, and thus to take the first step up the BCSM ladder. Empathy is one of those words whose meaning has been blurred by overuse, and nowadays it is used almost as a synonym for sympathy. So it is just worth returning to basics and the *Oxford English Dictionary*, which gives the following definition: 'The power of projecting one's personality into, and so fully understanding, the object of contemplation'.

So achieving empathy in a negotiation does not mean sympathising with your counterparty. How can you sympathise with a dangerous terrorist who is threatening to carry out some unspeakable act? But it does mean stepping into their shoes and understanding their view of the world.

In circumstances in which your negotiating counterparty is fanatical or disturbed, empathy is extremely hard to achieve. This is because there is no such thing as an emotional vacuum. Even the most mundane negotiations swim in emotions that are the residue of earlier experiences or have resurfaced as a result of this particular conversation.

If you have the emotional intelligence to understand their outlook, you can frame your communication with them so that it is as effective as possible. That understanding provides the platform on which you can build rapport and move towards a position where you can influence behaviour.

Body language

I touched on body language in Chapter Two, when I referred to the usefulness of physical messages when observing whether information is being presented effectively to different personality types. This fascinating subject, which has only been systematically researched in recent years, deserves a book of its own. Indeed, one that I would recommend as an excellent introduction to the subject in the context of business is Allan and Barbara Pease's *Body Language in the Workplace*.

To the untutored, body language is an unconscious communication. That is the reason why it can be such a powerful tool for those who take time to understand and control it. It can reinforce a verbal message and make the recipient of your communication believe more strongly what you are saying. Or it can contradict the spoken message and thus undermine what you are trying to say. And, in the absence of words, it can speak on its own.

The importance of first impressions has almost become a cliché. But there is no doubt about it; research shows that people will form as much as 90 per cent of their opinion of you in the four minutes after their first meeting. Around three-quarters of this opinion will be derived from non-verbal sources.

Handshakes

Often the first contact we make is the handshake. A damp, floppy, wet-fish handshake is deeply off-putting and projects a lack of confidence. An excessively firm, bone-crunching handshake will raise the hackles because it hurts (especially if the recipient is wearing rings) and gives the impression that the bone-cruncher wishes to dominate the other shaker. Even the orientation of your hand has an impact; if you tip the handshake so that your hand is on top, it will give the impression that you are trying to dominate. If you accept this position, or twist your hand underneath, you will give the impression of subservience. So if you wish to develop a quick equal rapport via your handshake, keep your hand vertical and deliver firm but not hard pressure.

Most importantly, you should be alert to the pressure that you receive in return and adjust your grip to return a similar pressure.

I SEE WHAT YOU ARE SAYING

In fact, it is another example of the mirroring behaviour that I touched on in Chapter Two. Then, of course, there are cultural differences that you should take into account. Americans will tend to pump their handshakes several times. Germans expect a once up and down movement. Many Continental Europeans may expect a handshake every time they meet you; to a Briton that may seem strange. Japanese may prefer not to shake hands at all. It is all about adjusting your behaviour to what will make the person you wish to impress most comfortable.

Appearance

Then there is the way you look. In some ways, of course, you cannot help your appearance. And in some ways you can, by doing your best to remain fit and healthy, and being well-turned out. This does not mean being obsessively neat or wearing a business suit to every meeting. If you wish to do business with a software company where everyone wears T-shirts and jeans, a suit may well create a barrier; visiting a banker in your T-shirt and jeans may not result in the loan you want (unless you are a successful software entrepreneur!). Either way, overloading your pockets or arriving with an overstuffed briefcase are mistakes that will give the impression of disorganisation.

The best position

Whether sitting or standing, the best position from which to build rapport is often at 45 degrees to your counterparty. Sitting or standing directly opposite someone is a more aggressive position and is more likely to lead to conflict and disagreement. If you are too close to a person, invading their body space, you can make them feel uncomfortable; if you are too far away, you may seem distant or weak. Again, cultural differences have their part to play here; typically, Japanese will feel more comfortable standing closer to other people than Americans, for example.

Controlling your movements is important. High-status

individuals tend to sit still and to use fewer gestures. This will give the impression of calm and self-confidence. Fiddling with objects – pens, parts of your clothing or parts of your body – has a very negative effect because it conveys nervousness, lack of confidence and even lack of sincerity. Looking your counterparty in the eye is important to convey sincerity and attention, although holding your counterparty's gaze in a fixed way throughout a meeting is likely to begin to feel aggressive and even hostile. Once again, mirroring is often the key; look a person directly in the eye to the same degree that they are looking at you.

One interesting technique if you wish to stop someone in their tracks or assert your authority is the 'power gaze'. This involves looking fixedly at a point equidistant between the bridge of their nose and the centre of their forehead. Narrow your eyes and focus without blinking. This is intimidating because it mirrors the attitude of many predators before they strike. This technique can have the effect of silencing the person you are communicating with and forcing them towards submission.

Giveaway gestures
There are some giveaway gestures of which it is useful to be aware. Folded arms, or arms held in front of the body, suggest defensiveness and lack of receptiveness. If someone covers their mouth when they are speaking, it can indicate that they are not telling the truth or at least are uncomfortable with what they are saying. Research has also shown that even people who are good at controlling their body language are likely to start moving their legs around when they are lying. Indeed, leg positions and movement can generally be very telling. Uncrossed legs tend to indicate an open attitude; crossed legs can indicate resistance or uncertainty. If someone is sitting with their legs pointing towards the door or the exit, it may mean that they do not feel involved, and wish to end the meeting and leave. If the person you are talking to puts his (and this *is* normally a male gesture) hands behind his head, it indicates a sense of superiority and a feeling that he has the answers – not a sign you necessarily

want to see if you are negotiating with him.

Eye movements can be revealing. Research into neuro-linguistic programming – NLP, for short – suggests that split-second unconscious eye movements expose what is going on in the brain. For example, when someone's eyes flick upwards they are probably recalling a picture or an image. This may indicate that they prefer to be communicated with visually and will respond well to being shown a picture or a chart. If the eyes flick down towards the right, they are probably recalling a feeling or an emotion, and if to the left, they are probably thinking a point through. Reading NLP correctly is complex (for example, right-handed and left-handed people behave in different ways) and requires considerable training. But it may be an area that you might be interested to investigate further.

MORE PIES please

I enjoy the 'More Pies' acronym because it fits so well with the subject. The acronym describes eight conversational techniques that help us to communicate and negotiate well. Some we are likely to use instinctively as a matter of course, but if we really understand these techniques and adopt them consciously, we will succeed in more negotiations ... and get More Pies:

- **M**inimal encouragers – brief responses to show the other person that you are listening and to keep them talking, such as nods, grunts, words and phrases such as *really, well, I see*.
- **O**pen-ended questions – questions that require responses of more than a simple yes or no for drawing out the responder, often prefixed with words such as *who, what, where, why, how*.
- **R**eflecting/echo questions – brief follow-up statements that repeat the speaker's last few words or word and allow the speaker to continue or clarify, such as *'Angry?'* in response to the statement: *'I know they hate me because they get so*

angry.'

- **E**motional labelling – a fast route to building empathy by identifying the emotional aspect of a statement and acknowledging it by labelling it correctly, such as: *'I feel that you are very angry because you have been misunderstood. However, your anger shows how passionate you are and that shines through.'*
- **P**araphrasing – a brief restatement of the speaker's point in your words: *'So you think they dislike you because you get cross.'*
- **I** questions – a three-part process allowing you to endorse positive behaviour and challenge negative behaviour without blaming the subject and indeed making it your own problem: *'I feel that you get angry … when you are misunderstood … because you are very passionate about things.'*
- **E**ffective pause – a powerful tool to be used immediately before or after saying something important. Furthermore, it helps to slow the conversation down, allowing you more time to think. It may also be used to show the other party that conversation is a turn-taking process. Silence may also be a good response to poor behaviour by the other party.
- **S**ummary – a periodic review of the main parts of a conversation to ensure that you have captured the salient points and emotions in your words. You should signpost your intention at the start: *'I would like to recap our discussion to this point. You are very angry because you have been misunderstood, but this is because you are very passionate about things.'* Then always finish with: *'Have I understood this correctly?'*

Trust

Trust is a vital component of any negotiation. Without trust you cannot build rapport. The conversational techniques listed above may help you to build rapport, but they will have no effect in the absence of trust. Trust requires honesty in order to flourish and therefore one of the most important things that you must strive for in negotiation is to never tell a lie. Experience shows that even the most difficult of individuals is prepared to accept a harsh truth in preference to a soft lie. However, the way you deliver that harsh truth is a matter of packaging. One of the most effective methods is to hold up a 'mirror of reality' to them.

For example: 'So am I clear, you are asking me for a coach so that you can drive off with the hostages? If you were in my shoes, would you let a person with a machine gun and explosives drive around this city?' By responding to their demand in this way you can avoid the need to lie.

Consistency in a negotiation is also an important element in building and maintaining trust and rapport. People like others to behave in a consistent, predictable way. Indeed, they often prefer individuals who are consistently unpleasant to those who are nice one moment and horrid the next. So, for example, most people can work with a poor boss, but they find it intolerable to have a boss who bullies them one minute and asks them out for a drink the next.

Negotiating techniques

Nevertheless, the need to maintain trust and avoid untruths does not mean that you should not use the tricks of the negotiating trade. What it does mean is that it is a poor negotiating technique to use the tricks of the trade in an utterly untruthful way. If you do, and are found out, or if your bluff is called, you will be placed in a very weak and vulnerable position, as well as damaging any rapport you may have built up with your opposite number.

Below are some of the tools you should carry in your kitbag.

Mutual problem solving

In a negotiation in which the objective of both sides is a win–win, and there is a commitment and desire on both sides to conclude a deal, the mutual problem-solving approach is generally the most effective. It has the merit of generally lessening the to-ing and fro-ing in a negotiation and thus reducing the time and effort required to reach agreement. This is because both sides are trying to understand each other's objections to a deal and to overcome those obstructions in a creative and collaborative way. It is also likely to cement the relationship between the two parties because their collaboration begins before the deal is even struck. If the deal is going to result in a long-term relationship, and the negotiation is about the terms and conditions of employment, say, or about a long-term investment in a business, or an acquisition where the management team in the target company will be an important element going forward, a negotiation based on anything other than a mutual problem-solving approach could be damaging to the extent of destroying the ultimate purpose of the deal.

The starting point

Judging correctly the starting point in many negotiations depends largely on how well you have prepared. You need to have equipped yourself with a comprehensive knowledge of the market in which you are operating, and an understanding of the prices and terms of things similar to what you wish to buy or sell. You also need to have fixed clearly in your own mind the minimum price you are willing to accept, or the maximum price that you are willing to pay. If you are fortunate, you may have been able to ascertain what your offering is really worth to your counterparty, how they are likely to react during the negotiation and how far they may be willing to move from an initial position. Whether or not to open the negotiation or to wait for the other side to do so is often just a matter of personal preference. The trick is to pitch your opening position further from the point that is acceptable to you than your opponent's opening position, as the to-ing and fro-ing that will follow will tend to settle near the mid-point between the two starting points. However, if you pitch the starting point too far away from a solution that is acceptable to both sides, you run the risk of destroying the negotiation before it has even begun and of driving your counterparty away without engaging them.

Win-win

I was recently in the Middle East to negotiate a large contract to provide security for a new oil field and to protect an associated pipeline. The meeting was held in a spectacular new seaside hotel. In spite of the modern surroundings, our Arab counterparties were dressed in traditional flowing robes, and, constrained by my jacket and tie, I felt rather jealous of their comfort.

When I heard their negotiating starting point my discomfort increased further. Their position was so extreme that it threatened to derail the negotiations before they had even begun. They wanted a price at least three times lower than the very best viable price we could offer. Fortunately, I had discussed this eventuality with my colleagues before the meeting began. We had undertaken extensive research about the group we were meeting and had also made a point of speaking with a number of people who had dealt with them in the past. This was invaluable as they had given us a blow-by-blow account of their initial meetings and how the relationship developed over a period of time.

So from what we knew of these individuals, we had anticipated the possibility of a completely unreasonable opening position. We were therefore ready with all the information necessary to demonstrate that their starting point was commercially unviable for us without them losing face as a result.

Because we were honest about our commercial position, we established a position of trust in response to their very first opening gambit. We knew this would strengthen the relationship because they were actually very astute commercially and could immediately see that their position would be refused. The ultimate benefit was that we struck a very fair deal that enabled both groups to walk away feeling they had achieved a success in the negotiation. This has also resulted in a strong relationship based on trust and respect whereby other projects have been brought to the table as a result of this initial meeting.

Reciprocity and concessions

Once the starting points have been established, the process of giving and extracting concessions begins. When you offer concessions, they should be made grudgingly and they should be small enough not to make your previous position look ridiculous. It is often desirable to make conditional concessions: *'I will give you what you ask, if you give me that in return.'* And making concessions that matter little to you – but are more important to your counterparty – will help to move you towards the territory of a win–win outcome. But of course you do not show that these concessions are 'easy gives' and mean little to you.

It is sometimes said that the golden rule of negotiation is that you should never make a concession without receiving one in return. Often this is correct, but there may be occasions when making a free offer of something that is important to the opposite party is the correct approach. Freely giving something without asking for something in return can create a strong desire and moral pressure to return the favour at a later stage.

Repetition

Unlike in the word game 'Just a Minute', repetition is an entirely justifiable tactic in negotiation and can serve to both underline the importance of a point to you and wear down the opponent's resistance. However, do not use it to a point where it becomes more irritating than effective. Saying the same thing again and again may eventually become counterproductive and provoke similar intransigence in your counterparty.

Silence

Making no response at all when your opponent makes an offer or a suggestion can be a powerful way of extracting some more information. Sometimes, giving no response, to a suggested price for example, but just sitting with a sad or slightly aggrieved expression on your face can result in a better offer without further ado. A tactical silence will generally work best if your counterparty is an Extrovert type. It is often said that salespeople tend to be Extroverts and buyers Introverts, so that silence can work well as a buying technique for the unwary or inexperienced salesperson.

Lack of authority
Perhaps slightly paradoxically, owning up to a lack of authority in a negotiation can strengthen your position, especially if there is time pressure to conclude the deal: *'I am sorry, but I am not allowed to agree to that. I will have to consult with my colleagues/my boss/go back to my committee.'* Quite often this will prompt the response: *'Fine, that doesn't matter too much, let's get on with it.'* On other occasions it creates the opportunity to consult either genuinely or artificially, and to return to the fray on a later occasion either with a regretful but entrenched position or offering a generous, hard-fought concession – in return for a *quid pro quo*, of course.

Good cop/bad cop
I talk above about the need to behave consistently during a negotiation in order to maintain trust. Yet sometimes it is important to bring pressure to bear on your opponent by being hard or unreasonable. The classic way to achieve this without prejudicing the rapport you have gained is the 'good cop/bad cop' routine. You are the good cop – warm, friendly, sympathetic, keen to find a win–win solution that works for both sides. You use a colleague to join the negotiation as the bad cop, who adopts a much more aggressive and hostile stance towards your opponent than you do. You push back against your colleague's harsh attitude. Done well, this has the effect of strengthening the tie between you and your opponent, while underlining to your opponent the difficulty you face yourself in persuading your colleagues or superiors to agree the position that your opponent is seeking.

Salami slicing
Salami slicing involves extracting a concession from your opponent by implying that if they make that concession you will conclude

a deal. Then, when the concession is granted, you make another demand, again backed by the implication that this is the final concession before agreement. And so it can go on.

In order to counter salami slicing, try to extract a full list of all the terms that the other side wishes to negotiate at the start, and keep all the terms interlinked. If an unacceptable number of slices are being taken off the salami, the best response is generally to say that you will consider the new concession that is being requested, but that all the other concessions you have made are now off the table.

External influencers

Invoking external influencers can be a useful technique in stoking your counterparty's enthusiasm to do a deal:

- *Authority* – The endorsement of third-party authorities in a negotiation can be a powerful influencer: *'Professor May-Smith's research demonstrated beyond doubt that this food will improve your cat's teeth.'*
- *Social proofing* – People are influenced by others they consider to be like themselves: *'9 out of 10 cat owners say their cats prefer this cat food and that it has improved their pets' dental health.'*

Threat of competition

Raising the spectre of your opposite number's main competitor can be remarkably effective: *'Yes, as a matter of fact I am talking about buying from/selling to your main competitor.'* Or you can plant the suspicion that such a conversation is going on by dropping a name casually into the conversation, or leaving a brochure or business card 'accidentally' displayed in your file or meeting room.

Scarcity

The old tag line 'buy now while stocks last' emphasises two types of scarcity – of the product itself, and of time in which to buy it. Both are valid in a market where supply is genuinely limited or where timescale is important. Where there are no such limits, invoking scarcity will be hollow and ineffective.

Feints

In order to distract your opponent's attention from your 'must haves', or perhaps even more so from the 'nice to haves' to which you attach the most value, you can use the 'feint' technique. Here, you argue strongly and at length for something that you do not really want very much, and that you know you will be unable to get. After a long discussion you sigh, point out to your opponent that he is unwilling or unable to make the concession you want, and ask for the thing that you really want instead.

Questions

Adapting the way you ask questions to different stages of a negotiation is a powerful way of moving things forward:

- **Open questions** – typically useful in the early stages of a negotiation when you are still primarily attempting to elucidate information and understand your opponent's position. Open questions start with words like *why, who, what, where, when* or *how* and can prompt a wide range of responses: '*Why did you climb up onto this roof?*'
- **Closed questions** – generally more aggressive than open questions because they demand a yes/no, true/false answer. Useful when you are trying to move an issue towards closure: '*Do you see that ambulance down there?*'
- **Tag questions** – a more subtle form of closed question where a phrase like *isn't it* or *aren't they* is tagged on to the end of a sentence: '*It's a long way down to the ground, isn't it?*'
- **Leading questions** – push the person being questioned towards the answer that the questioner wants them to

give: *'Before you decided to come up here and kill yourself, you thought about some other options, didn't you?'*

- **Presuppositions** – appear to offer a choice while attempting to narrow the options: *'Are you going to climb down the same way you came up?'*
- **Conditional questions** – offer the chance to consider options: *'I know that you are not ready to come down yet, but when you are, do you think you will climb down the same way you went up?'*
- **Partial agreement requests** – help to move the counterparty towards making a commitment: *'Promise me that you will think about the safest way down from the roof.'*

Recognising buy signs

If you are able to spot buy signs, then it often becomes possible to exploit them. Typical buy signs in a negotiation include the counterparty:

- asking a lot of questions: *'What would happen if we did it like this?'* or *'Do you think that you could guarantee this price?'*
- becoming silent, and asking for time to think about something or to confer.
- becoming less certain and changing or adding to their justification.
- asking for new concessions: *'I now need to take legal advice'* or *'If I agree to do this, will you promise to do that?'*
- moving away from conflict or disagreement towards compliance or agreement.
- showing signs of humour.

The power of 'because'

Behavioural scientist Ellen Langer and her colleagues decided to put the persuasive power of the word *because* to the test. In one study, Langer arranged for a stranger to approach someone waiting in line to use a photocopier and simply say, 'Excuse me, I have five pages. May I please use the Xerox machine?'

Faced with the direct request to cut ahead in the queue, 60 per cent of the people were willing to grant the stranger's wish. However, when the stranger added a reason to the request ('May I please use the Xerox machine because I'm late for a meeting and desperately need these documents for it?'), 94 per cent complied. That is probably what you would expect – most people like to help if they can – but here's where the study gets really interesting.

Third time around, the stranger also used the word *because* but followed it with a completely spurious reason: 'May I please use the Xerox machine because I have to make copies?' The rate of compliance was 93 per cent.

Remember to listen

My one regret in this area is teaching negotiation to my daughters. They have become so skilled in the art that I have to be awake to their individual tactics in extracting concessions. Now, even when I am home, I have to be alert to a well thought through negotiation. At least it keeps me on my toes!

I hope that you have found this chapter useful. As I said above, one possible negotiating technique is repetition, and I am going to avail myself of it here:

> If you choose to take only one thing from this chapter, it is that the key to successful communication and negotiation is to listen.

Let me close with two things that I like from two different cultures. I like the Native American proverb that says, 'Listen or thy tongue will keep thee deaf'. I also like the Chinese character for 'to listen':

Its component parts are illuminating:

眼 eyes [I see this as relating to focus and observation]

一 unity [in my view, focused attention is a vital part of listening]

心 heart or mind [which should be reflective and non-judgmental when listening]

耳 ears

So what?

It is useful to master the tricks of the negotiating trade, not least so that you can recognise them when they are being used by your opponent. However, they pale into insignificance beside the simple triumvirate of thorough preparation, effective communication and active listening. And in any event, do not allow the tricks of the trade to obstruct the development of the trust that is an essential ingredient in a successful win–win negotiation.

Generally, it is right to prepare for every negotiation in a way that is proportionate to its significance. An important negotiation deserves proper preparation, refining your objectives, rehearsing your position, planning your tactics with your colleagues and researching your opponent. But it is also worth remembering that every communication has the potential to become a negotiation.

Above all, listen actively to what your counterparty has to say. Put yourself in their shoes; develop the empathy to understand as far as possible why they are saying what they are saying, because that empathy will lead you towards the best response.

CHAPTER FIVE

Training yourself: getting into the flow

Excellence is an art won by training and habituation. We do not act rightly because we have virtue or excellence but we rather have those because we have acted rightly. We are what we repeatedly do. Excellence, then, is not an act but a habit.

Aristotle

The more I practice, the luckier I get.

Gary Player

'Behind enemy lines'

'By the time that the Delta Nine boys were climbing into their plane, Delta Eight had been driving for six hours in their Land Rovers. Have you ever been in the desert at night?'

'Well, yes, a few times on holiday.'

'Then you'll know how spectacular it can be. The light has a strange quality about it. If the moon is full you can often see very clearly, but you cannot see much colour. I know it's a bit of a cliché to call the moonlight pale and silvery, but that's exactly what it is like. And somehow it bleaches out all the colour. So Delta Eight had no problem seeing where they were going. On a couple of occasions when clouds did obscure the moon, it became more difficult (this was the era before night-vision goggles, remember); of course they did not have their headlights on, or show any other lights for that matter.

107

'Staff Sergeant Martin was in the second vehicle, in the back seat with Geordie, who was one of the radio operators. Colin, one of the other new guys, was driving. Next to him was Wings, one of the old hands. They planned to swap over every two hours. The patrol commander would always travel in the second vehicle because that made the most sense in case of an ambush. The corporal – Tom – was in the back seat of the first Land Rover, with the other three guys organised so that those with relative inexperience were next to someone who had been in the Regiment for longer. They kept up a steady pace. Going too fast carried too great a risk of hitting a rock or a boulder, and of throwing up an obvious plume of dust. They had another eight hours' driving time before they needed to find a place to hide up during the following day, so they would get close enough to the MSR to be able to swing into action the next night. They knew that the closer they got to the MSR, the more people were likely to be around, both civilians and military, so it was too risky to hide up too close to their ops zone anyway.

'The driver kept a close eye on the compass in the dashboard and maintained a steady bearing. Whoever was up front beside him also watched the compass. It wasn't that they were worried that the driver would not do his job properly – quite the opposite in fact; these guys really trusted each other – but it was just good practice to check and double-check everything. Every so often it was necessary to do a dog-leg to avoid ground that was too broken or boulder-strewn, or to skirt round the occasional gully. After these deviations, both front men checked the compass with special care. A bit of lateral movement did not matter because they were approaching the MSR from a perpendicular angle, and it was not too important precisely where they hit it.

'Far from being frustrated by these forced detours, Martin grunted with satisfaction and commented to Geordie beside him, "If the terrain continues like this, we won't have any problem finding an excellent LUP well away from prying eyes."

'Over to the east they could hear the intermittent roar of

planes dropping their bombing loads, and occasionally made out anti-aircraft. Once they heard the noise of a low-level plane and stopped so that their movement did not attract unwanted attention. Martin looked up. "Sounds like one of ours," he stated quietly to no one in particular.'

'Delta Nine?' I asked.

'Delta Nine,' Floyd agreed. 'But Delta Eight did not know that. Delta Eight knew nothing about what Delta Nine was up to. Need to know only, remember?

'The night passed without further incident, and Delta Eight progressed according to plan. Around 0400 hours Martin conferred briefly with Geordie and leant forward to speak to Colin, who was back behind the wheel again. "Okay, it's about ninety minutes before dawn starts to break. Time to find our LUP for the day. Catch up with the others."

'Colin picked up speed and came level with the first Pinkie. Both vehicles halted. A brief conversation took place.

'"Let's investigate the next gully we come to."

'"How about over there to the left?" Tom pointed to a low line of higher ground 400 metres away. "There might well be some folds; we could tuck ourselves away in there. And the higher ground could be a good vantage point for stag."

'"Good thinking, Carstairs." Without having to be told, Colin swung the vehicle round. Sure enough, as they approached the small ridge, they saw a rough canyon cut in the sandstone centuries before by water running off the higher ground. They eased the Land Rovers into the wadi.

'"Looks good," said Martin. Colin swung the Land Rover around in a U-turn so that it was facing out of the gully, and the second vehicle pulled up alongside. The team dismounted. Kevin was detailed to take the first two-hour stint of sentry duty and climbed to the higher ground, which provided a clear 360-degree view. Two of the others silently set up the camouflage netting. Then they all settled down to rest, their weapons near at hand.'

†

Get the basics right

One of the keys to success is to ensure that you do the basics well. All the best individuals are able to perform the basics under pressure. In the military, this might mean reloading your weapon quickly when you are under attack, following specific tactics and adapting them in adversity. In sport, it might be offloading the ball accurately to a teammate just as you are about to be tackled. In business, it might be answering effectively an objection from a sceptical potential customer. Or it might be something as simple as making sure that you create a good first impression when you walk into a room for a tense meeting – well turned out, a direct gaze, a correctly judged handshake – as covered in the last chapter.

Early in my military career, fairly soon after I joined the Paras, I was lucky enough to come under the command of a certain Al Slater. He was one of the best soldiers I ever came across – sadly I have to say 'was', because he was killed in an enemy ambush. He was an excellent trainer and became something of a mentor to me. It took a bit of time for me to appreciate him, because he always took a hard line on his command being the best group. He would put us through our paces on simple tasks again and again until we were the best without question. Back then I was impatient and often wanted to move on to the next thing quickly, but one thing that I learned from Al is that most people move on to the next thing too soon. Often, advanced training is no more than learning to do the basic things exceptionally well. In most areas people will talk about the basics but they rarely define them at an individual level, let alone as a team or an organisation. Doing basic things is repetitive and can lead to boredom, which is why people try to move on to other superficially more enjoyable elements as quickly as possible. However, doing basic things correctly in any of the fields in which I have worked is undoubtedly the first key to elite performance.

Mens sana in corpore sano

Many aspects of soldiering are physical, of course. You need to be fit. The same obviously applies to sport. I would not try to argue that you need the same level of physical fitness in business as in the military or a national rugby team. But there is no doubt in my mind that to perform well in business, or in any walk of life, you do need to attain and maintain a reasonable level of physical fitness. I don't mean that you have to be able to run thirty miles across rough terrain with a sixty-kilo pack on your back, but I do mean that you need to be fit enough to feel well, energetic and alert. Your brain, after all, is a physical organ in your body, and it will tend to function better if the other organs in your body are also working well and giving it the support it needs. In Chapter One we explored some of the very direct physical effects of the viscera on the brain, for example in the flow of stress hormones via the vagus nerve. To think of body and brain as separate entities is a mistake: the brain is part of the body and affected by many of the same physical things.

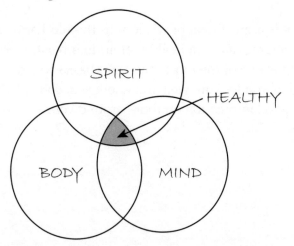

EVERYTHING'S CONNECTED: THESE
THREE THINGS NEED TO WORK
TOGETHER AND BE IN BALANCE

With mental toughness and the right attitude the brain can overcome great physical disadvantages. I think here of Professor Stephen Hawking, or of the extraordinary bravery of men and women who have lost limbs in the service of their country. For many of these heroes, pain is a constant presence that requires a continuous effort to control and overcome.

But there is no point in obstructing yourself with unnecessary handicaps. If you are in the fortunate position of not having to expend energy overcoming physical disabilities, do not allow yourself to get into a shape whereby you have to start doing so. An unnecessary lack of fitness makes it harder to achieve what you need. Give your body – and thus your brain – the dietary fuel that it needs to function well. You do not deliberately fill your car with low-octane leaded petrol when it runs best on high-octane unleaded. Look after your body – and thus your brain – by providing it with the rest and relaxation that it needs. And exercise both body and brain often enough so that neither lets the other down. If you do have any physical problems, do not worry about the things you are unable to do but concentrate on the things you can do.

There is a great deal of wisdom in the old Latin saying '*mens sana in corpore sano*' – a healthy brain in a healthy body. Getting this right is one of the most important basics to which I have just referred. If you look fit, well and energised, you will immediately make a good impression on those around you.

Time to step into the pressure zone

It was a bitingly cold wintry morning with a northerly wind blowing down the river against the flow of the water at Henley-on-Thames. Following heavy rain overnight, the river was high and swollen, the water choppy. I was on the riverbank outside the most prestigious and successful rowing club in Olympic history. Leander stands as a symbol of elite performance and personifies what it takes to be best in the world. Over one hundred gold medals since 1908 (not including the 2012 Olympics); the only pictures that adorn the walls inside the club are those of winners. You do not get a mention for second place. I took a deep breath to fill my lungs and calm my thoughts. I had been a soldier for most of my adult life and tested in every area of conflict over the last 27 years. I was about to leave my chosen profession and was looking to move into the area of psychology and performance coaching and teach what it took to perform at the highest levels not only in my own profession but in many others.

Today was an opportunity to give a talk to Olympic and World Champions and those wishing to emulate them about what I believed it took to perform at the highest levels when it mattered most. It was to be a trial run-through in a daunting environment. A great opportunity.

I stood still and thought for a moment. It struck me that for the first time in ages I was about to do something I was not good at nor fully prepared for. I had asked the head coach if I could train with the athletes beforehand to get a feel for what they actually did. So I was going to row in an eight with some of the greats; but I had never rowed in an eight before. No matter how well I performed, I would not be as good as the athletes I was about to row alongside. The coach took me round the building introducing me to everyone from the secretaries to the bar staff to the administrators. I was immediately struck by the tangible atmosphere of energy and professionalism in the club. As I walked into the gym I could also feel an electrical field of high performance in an arena that did not tolerate the thought of losing.

My performance that morning was crucial. My credibility was most definitely at stake. I was due to give them a talk later in the day on elite performance and elite environments. 'Hmm,' I thought to myself.

One of the Leander coaches stepped next to me as our boat was being lifted into the water. He confirmed that seven Olympic rowers plus myself would race against the up-and-coming development squad to ensure that we had a competitive element.

'There will be no quarter given today,' he added. As if I would have thought anything different! I could see him smiling to himself as he walked away.

'Thanks!' I said. I thought to myself for a moment and my internal voice added to the coach's comment, 'You will have to perform at the highest levels today.' My internal voice continued, 'You are not the leader today, but you must lead yourself. Don't think, just do; trust yourself.'

It was time to see if I could perform when it did matter. My mind skipped over the possibilities. If I made a mistake, what would they think about me as an expert on elite performance? 'Hmmm,' I wondered again, and I smiled inwardly as I knew the answer to that question. My heart began to beat a little quicker, and my mind started to focus on what I needed to do. I began my mental preparation cycle. My internal voice sounded again: 'What a great opportunity to see how good you are today, Floyd.' I love it when my mind hits the correct note and tells me that this is indeed an opportunity, not a possible failure to fear. We climbed into the boat and I was placed in the middle, at number five (where I could cause the least damage, perhaps?). I had a current Olympic champion in front of me and a future one behind me.

We started to pull away from the side. This team did not want to lose to the junior boat, that was for sure. Their banter made that crystal clear. We got into a nice rowing rhythm and made for the start line. The junior team were excited as they pulled up towards us and the banter continued. How they also wanted to win! Then the banter started to die down as we were brought alongside one another and each team prepared for the start.

We were given strict instructions from the support boat and we were brought into line; there was now absolute silence in both groups as the blades were placed into the water. We moved ourselves forward in the boat into the start position, and as soon as the boats were together we got the go and were off. I pushed my legs forward and pulled the oar through the water. We moved away very quickly and the stroke rate climbed rapidly; the plan I had prepared in my head kicked in. I had one single thought: 'JUST COPY the man in front, and follow his sequence exactly.' Under pressure I needed to think quickly, and to do that I had to minimise my conscious thoughts and any doubts.

Let's see if my theory worked. My heart rate was moving up and I was at my optimum level of physical and mental performance, but I just kept the single thought in my mind, 'Just copy, Floyd, just copy, don't think.' My focus was in the correct place: not in the future, not in the past, but absolutely in the now.

By the time we won the race the palms of my hands were bloody tatters. They'd blistered, burst and bled. I now noticed the pain. We'd won the race. I'd kept up with the Olympians. I'd done well.

'Well done, Floyd,' said the coach. 'I can see you have done a bit of rowing in your time.'

That was not the time to tell him otherwise and I simply said, 'Thanks.'

My talk later that morning went down quite well. I felt my new career had got off to a good start. And all I had done was concentrate on one simple thing – copying the others in the boat. And I also know that, even if I had 'failed', I would have done so seizing an opportunity.

Good practice

Whatever it is that you are training to do, it is vital to practise correctly. It is all too easy to cut corners, or to get a basic technique wrong, and to then practise mistakes. I call someone who practises well the perfect shape – a circle – because they have no corners to cut. In business, it is no different. I recently ran a training exercise for the safety, security and commercial success of a large sporting event. All of the stakeholders required to make this a success were gathered in the room. The basic elements were tested throughout the two days. The teams involved had different cultures, working practices and visions, but they had to learn to work together to become effective. The basics we worked on were:

- Defining the common purpose (a clear, unambiguous statement of intent).
- Defining the working conditions, measurements, culture and behaviours that were now expected.
- Ensuring we understood our own roles and those of others.
- Ensuring that communication, decision-making and accountability were clearly defined and practised.
- Ensuring that people took pride in working together and identified a code of conduct.

With basic principles in place, we then put these elements into practice by creating a live training environment where all of the skills necessary to make this a success were explained and practised. Once people exhibited the competencies, the groups were placed in a pressurised environment. There they were being judged on their ability to keep focused on the vision, their attitude towards one another, how they communicated and made a decision, and how they supported other groups in the decisions they made (in a pressurised environment they were still assisted if required). Later we started to test these elements and each group was marked on their performance, and, more importantly, we continued to do so (in a testing environment no external support is given).

For these things to become effective you have to learn to do them instinctively, without thinking, establishing the necessary templates in your brain, as we discussed in Chapter One. Then you can speed them up and introduce greater pressure to the training regime, reinforcing and strengthening what your brain has learnt. Overloading your brain to put it under pressure will reinforce those templates and make your actions more instinctive. This then means that, even in a pressurised environment, you feel comfortable and want to be there to test and challenge yourself.

Lack of training

Generally, in my experience, businesses and individuals in those businesses do not do nearly enough training. All too often, business people are just expected to get on with it without the necessary preparation. Or they are given some training and no opportunity to practise. Soldiers, sportspeople, musicians and public performers practise relentlessly to achieve excellence. The same principles should apply in business. Any meeting is a performance, and a sales presentation or conference speech even more so.

To practise effectively, and to make sure that you are not practising errors and cementing them into your performance, it is important to learn how to observe yourself from outside. Initially, this is likely to be best achieved by working with a coach, seeking peer-group feedback or watching video recordings of yourself in action. Once you really understand the techniques behind what you are doing, you can develop the self-awareness needed to assess your own performance impartially. Then you can begin to feel that self-awareness happen and see the result. A great idea is to keep a small video clip of yourself on your mobile phone, containing all of your best elements at work, whether that is performing a specific skill, training, speaking on stage or whatever. This enables you quickly to see all of the elements that allow you to perform at your very best and to remind yourself of them.

Taming your inner voice

Everyone has an inner voice in their head. You can turn this into a powerful internal coach if you really take control of it. A negative voice, or two or three competing voices, in your head will just sow confusion and doubt. Remember: the subconscious is not conscious of what is right and wrong or good and bad. It does what you, its owner, tell it to do. You need a single focus or vision that is clear about what you want to achieve, like a shining light that you can see no matter what the situation. This means you can always overcome doubt because you have the determination to succeed.

The voice inside your head is created by your experiences and how you have perceived those experiences. It is important to learn how to use your inner voice to harness the positive characteristics of those experiences and to turn them to your advantage. The first step is to move from fears and doubts about performing to seizing the opportunity to see how good you can be. Negative emotions will always take away energy. Fear, doubt and anxiety will not help you perform well. But it is quite possible to learn to turn those negative feelings into positives. Take, for example, how you view an audience. Your initial instinct, especially if your personality tends towards the introverted, is to get nervous because those people are watching you. Do they want you to hit a good shot, make a good speech or to fail and fluff your lines? Of course, they want you to entertain and excite them. They would prefer to see you succeed than fail. They are there to cheer you on. Learn to relish your audience; they are on your side.

Using stress

As we touched on in Chapter One, your reactions to situations such as being in front of an audience are based on physical triggers. Nervousness and stress cause your visceral organs to release the hormones adrenaline and noradrenaline. Through your vagus nerve, these hormones stimulate your amygdalae, those 'fight or flight' nodes sitting just in front of your reptilian brain at the top of your spinal column. The loop continues, with the signal being fed back to the viscera, releasing more hormones. Your brain can then flood with excessive dopamine, which potentially impedes your ability to control your body in the way that the situation demands. It may be great at helping you turn and run faster, or at flailing blows blindly at your enemy, but it will interfere with the fine motor skills that you have learnt and will thus impede your performance.

Controlling your breathing is an excellent way of regaining control of your body and your emotional responses. Think of a relaxing image. I think of a waterfall cascading over rocks, then of the word *focus* and then I take slow, deep breaths to get myself centred and relaxed. I use a count of between four and eight seconds to breathe in and breathe out if I need to calm my body and mind. As you know from Chapter One, your body is coded to react to your thoughts. In competition or in combat, your heart rate increases so that you are in the best state to perform. However, if you become too tense your heart rate can increase to a level that has this negative effect and interferes with your cognitive ability. This is where mental toughness comes in. By staying in control and learning to harness stress, you can achieve the right degree of tension in your body and ensure you are free to perform correctly when it matters most.

A success in psy-ops

Let me tell you a story about another girl, Rhiannon. She was about ten at the time, and had really got into shooting basketball hoops. One day she was practising in the same gym that some of my military friends use. One of them (I'll spare his blushes by not mentioning his name) saw her there. This friend of mine is supremely talented in a number of different sports and is one of the most able soldiers I have worked with. He hadn't seen Rhiannon there before but, being a friendly guy with kids of his own, he offered her a challenge.

'How about the first to ten hoops then?'

Rhiannon looked up at him and grinned wickedly. 'Okay, first to ten it is. I go first,' she said. She took the ball and stepped up to the mark. The ball looked really big in her small hands. She was totally focused, single-minded; she'd done this hundreds of times before. If you'd been watching you'd have thought she hadn't bothered to aim. Her arms swung and the ball looped and plopped satisfyingly through the hoop without touching the sides.

'Not bad at all,' said my friend, as he collected the ball and stepped up.

He was just about to throw the ball when Rhiannon's ten-year-old voice piped up, 'So I guess this is what you'd call a pressure shot now, isn't it?'

He turned his head to look at her. 'Unh?' She gave him a sweet smile. You could see the doubt creeping in.

He turned back towards the hoop, set himself, aimed carefully, threw … and missed by a mile.

Rhiannon sank each of her next nine shots in the same style. My friend missed every single one, his throwing getting wilder and wilder. Just as he was finishing, I walked back onto the basketball court to pick up Rhiannon, having finished my own training session. He clapped his hands to his head. 'I should have known she was your daughter, Floyd!' he said in mock despair.

Trigger switches

I find it helpful to use powerful words as trigger switches, words that really mean something to me and in which I have utter belief. Words such as *courage, determination, resilience, bottle*. If the word or a combination of words really means something, I can activate it when I truly need to. For example, I am on the eighteenth hole, I've played a poor approach shot and now I need to attack the green. I need courage. The green slopes left to right and downhill. When I go to hit the ball I must not think consciously about it anymore. I've made the decision to hit the brave shot, I know the lay of the ground and I know how hard to hit. I've done the training to enable myself to strike it right. I have visualised exactly what to do next; I can see the ball dropping into the hole. Now I just have to go in there and do it. It is time to trust myself. If you let a voice of anger, doubt, fear or complacency creep into your mind, your body will be affected as well.

Through the zones

I call the state of mind described in the previous section being in the 'red zone', the zone in which I stop thinking consciously and act. That is the zone for which you have trained yourself. You get to the red zone through three others. The first is the 'white zone', in which your brain may be occupied by multiple thoughts and not focused on any particular activity. You are in that zone when you do not need to focus on anything specific. The second is the 'green zone', in which you focus on the generality of the activity, in this instance the overall golf competition. It is important to activate the correct files in your mind relating to this activity. You should not be thinking about anything else that takes your focus away from this activity. The third is the 'amber zone', in which you are thinking about the specifics of a particular hole, the distance and your choice of club. Here, you refine the brain files you are activating. Then you are in the red zone, in which you just do it. Forget about the outcome; it will take care of itself. All you have to do is something you have done a thousand times. Trust yourself to do it.

When I am on my way to work as a soldier I will be thinking about all sorts of things: sport, relationships, politics and finance, with my mind flicking to and from each subject. However, as soon as I enter a military base I am thinking about being a soldier and what I am expected to do. This means that I am in the green zone, activating the correct files in my mind so that they are responsive to my needs. In the next zone, amber, I am concentrating on the detail of what I need to do, my role and the actual task. Then I enter the red zone and trust myself to react to anything that may occur.

The power of symbols

When I was in the Parachute Regiment, and indeed in the SAS, the colour of the beret and belt became powerful symbols of what I had achieved. Wearing them always gave me a sense of enormous pride and confidence because they symbolised the adversity I had gone through to win them. Other symbols can play an important part in strengthening your resolve. I often mark a red spot on my hand or wrist to look at every now and again. I use this as a symbol to help remind me to trust that I have the ability to perform the task at hand. If I commit myself to a timetable, I often use an hourglass as a clear indicator to remain focused on the task for the requisite length of time.

Cricketer Andy Flower, the 2012 winner of the BBC Coach of the Year Award, used to carry around a piece of paper with the number ten written on it. This represented his desire to be the tenth best batsman in the world rankings. Once he had achieved this, he took another piece of paper and wrote down the number one, symbolising his desire to be the world's top-ranked batsman. He achieved his goal, which was all the more extraordinary because he played for Zimbabwe, not a top-rank international side.

Commitment

None of this happens without commitment. I have seen some very talented people who just don't commit to performing excellently. Either they do not practise effectively or they do not prepare their bodies and minds to perform consistently on the biggest stages. Exceptional sportsmen like Rafael Nadal or Roger Federer have an outstanding level of mental toughness, not only because they are technically excellent, but because they prepare well. In them, mind, body and soul are united and therefore they are consistent in their approach to excellence. By training as you would compete in a real situation, by taking it as seriously as real life, you create a belief that this is your opportunity to succeed. There is no doubt in your mind that you deserve to be in the competition and will win even from a position of disadvantage. The key in relation to the mind, body and soul, or essence, is that they are in harmony and you are operating in the centre of all three. This leads to excellence in any activity.

Present and correct

In order to perform well, you must learn to spend time in the present and focus your energy and attention entirely on the immediate moment. Often you can become too focused on the future. You think ahead to 'what will happen if I win this point?' or 'won't I be a hero if I take this order?' Your attention then wavers from the present, you lose concentration, and the chance of achieving what you want reduces. You also spend too much time worrying about what happened in the past. 'Last time, I lost the point,' you think, or 'Last time, I did not get the order.' Of course you need to learn from the past. That is partly what training is about. But that lesson either needs to be learnt before you go into action again or set on one side to be addressed in your training and preparation for the next time. When you are in the middle of the action, you must stay in the 'now'.

It is possible to create positive anchors by remembering all the times that you've played well or been confident, courageous, motivated and determined. You can do this by 'imaging' those events and remembering what you saw, what you felt, what you smelt, what you heard. You will have felt a degree of stress when you experienced these events, so because of the workings of your brain it should be possible to recreate them with clarity. This enables you to feel again the positive emotions you experienced before and assists in minimising any doubt or uncertainty in your mind.

In sports training, I always try to get a video compilation of the person at their best. I want to emphasise to them why they are good and show them what I want them to continue doing. Of course I will also look at their limiting weaknesses one at a time and help them to eliminate them, but that is secondary. The primary goal is to remind them of their strengths. For business training, I always build a story board of success. I identify what a person has done well since they were young, what they have achieved, what behaviours helped and who helped them. I then get them to play these events in their mind so that they can call upon these positive attributes whenever they need them. The same principles work for teams.

Personal mastery

In order to master your emotions, you need to remember that they all come from inside yourself. Other people do not upset you; you upset yourself. External situations do not upset you. You only get upset when you lose control of yourself and allow external influences into your mind. From Chapter One you know what happens when you allow yourself to become frightened or nervous. Your brain and your body are interacting in a fundamental physical way. It is all about you, not about somebody else. To achieve personal mastery and self-control, you must always remember that it is down to you, not somebody or something else. It is internal, inside yourself, not external. When you are practising, there must be consequences for bad performance. Invoking a threat that is real makes the practice more effective by creating a certain amount of pressure. In sport, those individuals who do not complete a task or are in the bottom three during a particular challenge might have to take an extra skills session or extra physical training. In business, I would make a team carry out an additional project or presentation to create the correct amount of pressure to enhance the team's performance. These consequences are not intended as punishment, but to induce additional pressure before the event.

Boxing clever

I used to do a lot of boxing in my Army days. It was probably the sport that I loved most because I believe that it demands a higher level of fitness and stamina than any other activity. I remember one occasion when I was representing the British Police team (yes, the reason for that is a long story!). We were fighting the Royal Air Force and had travelled all the way to their base at RAF St Athen.

When we got there, I was told that there was nobody of my own weight to fight me. It really disappointed me that I had travelled two hundred miles to no purpose. The team had a wise old trainer, Fred McGlyn, who had known me for several years. He come up to me and said, 'Floyd, I think you will be pleased. Even though there is nobody at your own weight, they have got an opponent for you. He is big – a super-heavy – but you've fought bigger men before. Do you want to take him on?' Did I want to take him on? Of course I did. 'Yes, sure,' I said, pleased that my trip would not have been wasted. I had fought super-heavies before; generally they were two or three stone overweight, so the extra poundage did not make them more formidable opponents. I went to get changed. Both my father and grandfather had been boxers. It was my favourite sport and at this time I was unbeaten as a heavyweight.

I came back from the changing rooms to the welcoming ceremony. We walked into the arena and lined up opposite the RAF team. Now, for the first time, in front of a thousand spectators, I saw my opponent. He looked as tall, broad and hard as a tropical teak tree. He was a good four inches taller than me, with a reach to match, and he looked in peak condition. There was not an ounce of fat on him. His muscles were large and well defined. He looked a bit like one of those killer Russians in a Rocky movie and was definitely the largest human being I had ever seen.

I felt the blood draining from my face as I left the arena. I asked a mate to get the massive fighter's boxing card. I wanted to see how good he actually was. The news was not good: twenty-five fights, no defeats, twelve of the victories within the distance. This guy was the Combined Forces super-heavyweight champion. 'What on earth is he doing in the RAF?' I thought. 'The only plane big enough to get him off the ground is a Hercules.' 'Thanks,' I muttered nervously.

I wandered off to the other side of the changing room to feel sorry for myself. My confidence was now ebbing away; my body was beginning to feel tight. Did I have a cold coming on, I wondered, as I checked to see if my glands were up. My mind started to fill with other concerns about what everyone – my family, my friends – would say if I was beaten. Because I could only think negatively, I was activating all the wrong mental files with a negative effect on my body, which was not helping me at all.

Fred walked across the changing room after sorting out one of the other members of the team and whispered, 'What's the matter? Are you okay?'

'I've just seen his card. I think I might have bitten off more than I can chew this time.'

Fred nodded and paused for a moment. 'Why do you box, Floyd?' he asked.

I thought for a moment and answered simply, 'To see how good I can be.'

'Well, that's fine then, because tonight you get to see how good you really are.' Fred paused again while his words sank in. 'Let's look at what you have achieved before.'

He took me through all the fights I'd had against tough opponents. He told me to think about the hours of training I had undertaken. He pointed out that this arena actually suited my style, so that I had the advantage. He then made me focus on my game plan, talking about the basic drills for the fight, and the courage I would need.

'Of course he's a difficult opponent. He'll be a proper challenge, and at the end of the fight you really will know how good you are. There's nothing wrong in feeling a bit nervous; that is just your body coming alive to danger and getting you ready to react. There is no point in trying to hide it; work with it to your advantage. Once you admit to yourself that this will be difficult, you will start to concentrate on what you can do about it.'

My mind was back in sync with my body like a proper team. I did really want to see how good I could be. I felt disappointed in myself for allowing those negative thoughts to distract me and steal my energy. I took some deep breaths and got myself focused. By the time the cry 'Seconds out, Round One' came from the referee, I was ready. I was in the red zone and just trusted that I would know what to do.

It was one of the tougher fights of my life, but three rounds later he had not knocked me down and I had won a unanimous decision on points.

When I look back on my boxing career, I can see clearly that whenever I have lost, it has been because my mental preparation was inadequate.

RED CORNER, RED ZONE, READY

Getting into the flow

The ultimate objective of training and preparation is to get your mind and body into the perfect performance frame. From here, it is a short step to being 'in flow'. The concept of flow was originally proposed by psychologist Mihály Csíkszentmihályi. Csíkszentmihályi devoted much of his life to studying and researching 'optimal experience' and has written extensively about it. His 1990 book *Flow* provides the most accessible summary of his work.

In Csíkszentmihályi's language, flow is the mental state of operation in which a person doing an activity is fully immersed in a feeling of energised focus, full involvement and concentration on the process of the activity. He calls it flow because individuals who participated in his research often referred to the sensation in this way, with phrases such as 'It was like floating' or 'I was carried by the flow'. So flow is a completely focused motivation, a single-minded immersion in an activity, and represents perhaps the ultimate in harnessing the emotions in the service of performance and learning. In flow, the emotions are not just contained and channelled, but are positive, energised and aligned with the task at hand. Not only does flow mean that you are performing better; it also means that you are deriving more enjoyment from what you do. When you are in flow, you are comfortable and operating at your maximum potential, with your mind, your body and your self-belief in harmony, working seamlessly together for optimum performance. A hallmark of flow is a feeling of spontaneous enjoyment while performing a task.

Csíkszentmihályi's work examines the occasions when people perform at their best and derive maximum satisfaction from doing so. His objective is to identify the ingredients necessary to achieve flow. His research has not only looked at the more obvious instances of flow, such as a performance by a sportsperson or musician, but also at flow in mundane repetitive tasks that would normally be viewed as boring.

Effort

The first requirement of flow is effort. One of the sensations of flow may be that the activity feels effortless, but it nevertheless requires effort to get there. Flow cannot be passive in the way that some pleasures are – lying in the sun or watching a mindless television show. The enjoyment derived from flow is on a higher, active level. Swigging a glass of wine might provide pleasure, tasting a glass of wine with concentration, identifying the different flavours, working out the grape variety and perhaps where in the world it was made, takes the experience to a different plane of active enjoyment that could potentially involve flow.

Concentration

The second requirement is concentration. When your brain is relaxed and unfocused, a jumble of thoughts bubbles around and comes to the surface at random. Because of the way the brain works and the precedence it gives to stress-induced memories, these random thoughts tend to be your worries and concerns, such as things that you have not done and should have. A haphazard mental state is therefore not normally pleasurable. One reason that a passive activity such as watching mindless television can be pleasurable is that it diverts the mind from random worries and concerns and introduces an element of order. However, greater order, and therefore greater active enjoyment, comes from deep concentration when your thoughts, intentions, feelings and senses are all flowing in the same direction.

Challenge/skill balance

The third requirement is to achieve the correct balance between challenge and skill. If you do not feel you have enough skill for the task at hand, you are likely to experience anxiety. On the other hand, if you have too much skill, if the task is too easy, you may not operate at your best level because of boredom. If you can understand this balance and strike it right so that you feel neither too much anxiety nor too much boredom, you can maximise your performance more consistently. In my view, the way to achieve this balance is not by reining in your training or limiting the levels of skill that you attain, but rather by consistently increasing your levels of skill and maintaining your interest by entering the pressure zone again and again to stretch yourself further. It is always possible to do something better, and because being in flow is enjoyable it is a vital motivational element in training and getting better. Staying in the 'effort vacuum' will never get you into flow; stepping into the 'pressure zone' and improving your performance will. You cannot remain elite without continuous improvement; to remain elite, to continually get into flow, you have to get better.

Figure 4. The balance between challenge and skill; adapted from Csíkszentmihályi's book

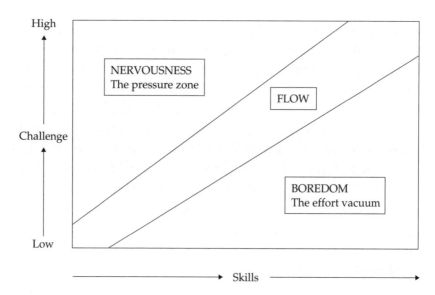

Goals

The fourth requirement is to have a clear goal in your activity, of course set at the right level to achieve the correct balance between the pressure zone and the effort vacuum. So in a race, the goal might be to win, but if the other runners are much better than you, the goal may be to beat your last time or just to finish. In tennis, you might want to win the game, but if your opponent is too weak for a victory to be an achievement your measure might be different – eliminating any double faults, or playing regularly and improving a shot that is not your best. In a business meeting, you similarly need to have a clear objective – to close a sale or to conclude a negotiation or to progress towards doing so.

Feedback and measurement

A fifth requirement of flow is some means of measuring how you are doing as you go along. In your race, this might be your lap time or your position against the rest of the field. In your tennis match, it might be the score, or your personal count of your double faults or the shot you wanted to hit. If you are performing in front of an audience as an actor, musician or public speaker, you will doubtless assess the level of applause at the end, but along the way you will monitor the audience's continuous feedback through their laughter, perhaps, or their attention. And in a business meeting, you will be measuring the feedback of the people with whom you are interacting in a similar way – via their verbal feedback and their body language.

It is worth noting that you can turn a mundane, routine activity into something with the potential for flow by attaching goals to it – soldering more circuit boards on a production line than ever before, or putting more letters into envelopes in a certain space of time.

Unity of purpose

When you are in flow, you do not feel separated from the event that you are experiencing. Instead, it is as if you are at one with the activity you are conducting. You are able to understand each moment because you have thought through each element or phase and can hit the goals or game plan you structured before the event. It also enables you to adjust throughout because you can react to the feedback you receive. Because of your crystal-clear concentration, you are aware of not only the detail around you but also your strategic intent. You perceive all of these factors in a positive way. In flow you have a sense of total control and feel as if you can do nothing wrong. You are free from any lack of confidence or fears that you may have.

Passage of time

It is possible to stay in flow for hours and remain focused. The whole thing becomes a virtuous circle. Time also takes on another dimension. People who are in flow often lose track of time. In some physical activities it can be as if the clock slows and you find that you have lots of time to make a decision or perform an action. Alternatively, an event that takes hours seems to be over in a flash. In flow, time can take on *Doctor Who* qualities. Once you have been in this flow and performed to your full potential, you will often enjoy a long feeling of euphoria.

One of the reasons why flow time appears elastic is because the brain can only process a certain amount of information at once. If you are totally focused on your flow activity, using your whole brain to concentrate on what you are doing, there may not be enough spare capacity to process something such as the passage of time.

I'M FLYING, NOT TIME

Negative emotions

You cannot achieve flow if you are beset with negative emotions. Boredom, fear, jealousy, anxiety and nervousness are all enemies of flow. So developing the mental toughness to banish these demons is an important part of learning how to achieve flow.

The first step is to accept that these negative emotions do exist. You have to learn to deal with them. Just denying their existence will mean that they pop up when you do not want them to. In Chapter One we talked about the inner workings of the brain and how to use the mind so that you are in full control of your body. So you now know that the effects of negative emotions are physical, chemical reactions that can be controlled. Reaching this understanding, the understanding that they can be controlled, is the second step.

Turning them to your advantage is the third step. If I feel nervous in the face of a challenge, I welcome that feeling because it tells me that my body is preparing to perform in response. But I never allow that feeling of nervousness to block out my ability to think. I remind myself that I have trained, practised and prepared for the challenge that I face. I know that I am ready for it and I make sure that my inner voice continues to tell me so. By refusing to allow the chemicals produced by negative emotions to flood the rational part of my brain, I retain the ability to adapt my game plan if my opponent is outmanoeuvring me in any particular area.

I also ensure that my picture of success, my visualisation of what I want to achieve, remains firmly in my mind. And I remind myself that failure cannot exist if I have done my utmost to succeed.

How to get into flow

Let me try to summarise how to get into flow more often:
1. Learn to step into the pressure zone as often as possible. See any challenge as an opportunity to learn from the experience. Relish the chance to perform to the best of your potential.
2. Remember that the biggest obstacle in getting into flow will always be yourself. Forget about others and how they see you; do not let doubts or negativity from them enter your mind. Just trust in yourself.
3. Set yourself clear and realistic goals in every element of your role, especially in training or preparation. Take advantage of any feedback and use it constructively. Also listen to your

body's feedback and what it is telling you; are you healthy and taking in the necessary food and liquid?

4. Always concentrate on what you have to do. Do not be distracted by what your competition is doing. Do not fight the environment you are operating in or allow yourself to be put off by it; it is the same for everyone.

5. Stay in the present by concentrating on your processes. In other words, forget about outcomes and just concentrate on what you are actually doing. Do not allow negative thoughts to invade your mind; concentrate on the positives. Don't worry about controlling time, because by simply being in flow, time will adjust to your individual needs, whether in speeding up or slowing down.

6. Effective and accurate feedback is essential. You need to identify your weaknesses in order to know where to improve.

7. Perhaps most important, remember to enjoy what you are doing. Enjoyment will free your creativity. Enjoyment turns flow into a virtuous circle.

Flow control

You control flow through your training. The more you practise a skill, the easier it becomes to perform it under extreme pressure. The more you perform it under pressure, the better you become, and the better still you can become. Using and controlling flow is an essential part of becoming and remaining elite.

I was once asked after a very tough day why I had made certain decisions and acted in the way I had. I paused for a moment before answering and realised that I had done all those things instinctively. I had not had to think consciously, yet I had been able to adjust and make clear, timely decisions. The difficult day had gone well and I was in a brilliant state of mind. I realised then that I had been in flow, that magical moment when you can do no wrong.

So what?

Basic training and careful practice can be a real grind. But it is a small price to pay for the glorious exhilaration of flow. If you have once experienced flow and achieved a truly outstanding performance, you will never again question the worth of that basic training. You will know for sure that it is has been a price well worth paying.

Whatever you do, whether it is sport, music, art, soldiering, business, those basics have to be mastered so well that they become instinctive. If you practise badly, and then practise mistakes, or if you move on too early, all your effort will be wasted.

Your inner certainty that you have mastered the basics to an instinctive level of excellence is vital to the mental toughness that you will need to achieve elite performance. That mental toughness feeds back into that certainty, creating a self-belief that in turn increases your mental toughness. It is a virtuous circle. But if there is any doubt in your heart of hearts about whether you have mastered the basics, any sneaking suspicion that you may have cut corners and moved on too early, that virtuous circle can reverse and turn vicious.

Teach yourself to focus exclusively on the present when you are performing. Understand the mix of ingredients you need to get into flow and strike the right balance between nervousness and boredom. Do this by pushing yourself further and taking on new challenges, by stepping back into the pressure zone every time it becomes too easy. Then you will derive maximum enjoyment from your activity, whatever it is.

CHAPTER SIX

You as part of a team

You cannot be a leader, and ask others to follow you, unless
you learn how to follow too.

Sam Rayburn

'Behind enemy lines'

'So Delta Eight are safely hunkered down? What about Delta Nine?'

'Yes,' said Floyd, grinning, 'although I don't think that
'"hunkered down" is exactly a military expression! But let me tell
you about Delta Nine.

'If you remember, they had broken into two teams. Jim had set
off north with Billy, Chico and Stu to recce towards the ops zone.
They just carried their A-frames, including enough food and water
for three days, in case.'

I chipped in. 'And their belt kit, of course. You never take that off.'

Floyd grinned. 'You're learning. So Stan, Jim's number two in
rank, stayed with Fletch, Evan and Gus to guard the rest of the
equipment. This equipment cache also included the only long-
range radio they had with them. If you remember, in order to save
weight Delta Nine had decided to take only one. Jim's group did
take one of the two low-wattage patrol radios, but these only had
a range of a couple of kilometres. So to all intents and purposes
the two groups would be out of contact with each other.

'The LUP they'd found wasn't great. The dry watercourse was
a bit too open, and now as the weather worsened it turned into
a funnel for the wind. Stan gave Fletch the first stretch of stag up

on the top of the outcrop and then settled down to try to rest with Gus and Evan. He couldn't resist a brief dig at Gus.

'"You kicked off a bit rough with Jim about the plan."

'"Yeah, I know. I'm sorry. I was just really frustrated. I knew that Stu had been in the desert before – he'd told me about the icy conditions he'd encountered. He's also a big reader – says that many of the explorers have described just the same weather. I was just frustrated that Jim hadn't drawn on his knowledge and got him to speak up. I know it's not easy with a quiet guy like that, but if he had we might be in a better place now."

'"I think you need to take a bit of the blame for that too, you know. You could've spoken up in a calm and measured way instead of showing your petulance."

'"I know. I've just apologised, haven't I?"

'Several kilometres north, Jim might have wished that this conversation about him behind his back really had made his ears burn, because instead they were freezing. The wind was now hurling sleet across the plateau almost horizontally into their faces. The trouble is, even when it's really cold, if you are carrying a thirty- to forty-kilo load, you sweat. Then, whenever you stop, the sweat chills you to the bone, sapping your energy and morale.

'Visibility was also getting worse. The team tabbed on through the murk for what seemed like an eternity. The ground alternated between long, flat, open stretches and shorter areas of broken ground. When necessary they fixed an ERV – emergency rendezvous – point where they would regroup if they had an enemy contact and became separated. Then, at last, they emerged from another rough patch and found themselves looking down a shallow slope. At the bottom, even through the sleet, they could see several sets of headlights moving roughly east–west ahead of them.

'Jim grinned. "The MSR. So it is within reach after all."

'"And there should be some good LUPs along this ridge."

'"Let's take a bit of a breather and then head back. We'll move the kit tomorrow night and then we can get to work."

'Jim, Chico, Billy and Stu rejoined the others around dawn, and Delta Nine spent another day in extreme discomfort because of the weather. Come mid-afternoon, the sleet stopped, visibility improved, and the temperature began to rise a little. As they were all soaked through by now, it did not help much; they almost looked forward to the night's exertions as a means of warming themselves up.

'As soon as it was dark, they set off on the bearing that Jim had followed the previous night. As on their first night, they moved the heavy equipment forward in relays. Their initial gratitude for the improvement in the weather turned rapidly to concern. The sky cleared and the moon illuminated the desert with a light that seemed almost as clear as day. Delta Nine were uncomfortably exposed on the long stretches of flat ground that they had to cover between ridges. With their heavy burdens they knew that it would not be possible to take cover rapidly. Their worst fears were realised when, a kilometre into a pancake-flat piece of ground, they heard a convoy of vehicles in the distance. The noise grew steadily and appeared to be coming straight towards them. The vehicles came into sight: a jeep in front, followed by two covered trucks, the menacing shape of a missile launcher of some type, another truck and a second jeep.

'"Cover," Jim hissed. "Let them by. If they show signs of seeing us and stop, open fire with me and withdraw. Leave the heavy gear except the radio. Regroup at the last ERV."

'Delta Nine made themselves as small as possible in the featureless landscape. They watched the direction of the enemy convoy. If it continued on its course, it would pass within twenty yards of their position. It seemed impossible that they would not be seen. Unconsciously every man held his breath. The convoy was halfway past when it ground to a halt. They heard a foreign voice give an order and two figures climbed from the front jeep.

'Jim waited no longer. The patrol opened fire. Shouts of surprise at the sudden assault were drowned out by gunfire. Accurately thrown grenades disabled two of the trucks. Enemy soldiers poured out of them like bees out of a damaged hive. Delta Nine began their withdrawal in relays, four men taking it in turns to lay down covering fire for the other four as they headed back towards the cover provided by the ridge a kilometre behind them. The rear jeep came after them, its fixed machine gun spraying bright bands of tracer through the night. An accurate volley of fire stopped it in its tracks. After that, the pursuers were more circumspect and kept their distance.

'At the ERV, Delta Nine regrouped. "We have to assume that with first light they'll come looking for us. We need to make as much ground towards the south as we can. Evan, get a signal out requesting an emergency pick-up at our drop-off point."

'Evan shook his head grimly at Jim's request. "The wireless took a round in the firefight. Knocked me off my feet. I suppose it saved my life, but it's no good for anything else."

"Right. Let's get a bit further south and make a decision from there."'

✝

Why be part of a team?

In Chapter One, when I was attempting to explain the wonderful workings of the human brain, I perhaps missed out an important point. Well, better late than never, so here it is. Why did the human brain develop from that basic reptilian model, wrapping itself in the second layer of paleomammalian brain to enable social nurturing behaviours, and then encasing that layer in the state-of-the-art neomammalian cortex? Why did we evolve in such a way?

Evolution is of course about survival of the fittest. So a key reason for the way our brains have developed is that we stand a higher chance of surviving and prospering if we have the emotional and social skills required to work with other members of our species – in other words, to work in a team. The whole point of working in a team is that you can achieve more as part of a group than when working solo. Let me put that in a more selfish way. The whole point of working in a team is that you can achieve more *for yourself* as part of a group than when working solo. So there is a fundamental contradiction inherent in working in a team: you are doing it to benefit yourself in a selfish way, yet in order to generate the maximum possible benefit from team-working you have to become selfless and subsume that selfishness in the greater good. That inherent contradiction is one reason why working well in a team requires training and practice.

But it is worth the effort. Good teamwork is enlightened self-interest.

GOOD TEAMWORK GIVES YOU A LIFT

Life or death

In any branch of the military, whether or not a team functions effectively can be a matter of life and death for its members – in the literal sense, of course, not just metaphorically. A slip by one member of the team can imperil not just their own physical survival, but that of all the other members of the team as well. That is one reason why so much time is dedicated to training to ensure that military teams function correctly.

As is clear from Chapter Five, some military training, indeed a lot of military training, is specific to the tasks that we expect to face. Learning how to wield an Armalite will not, one hopes, be a useful skill on the sports field or in the boardroom. But as I hope Chapter Five also makes clear, the principles behind training are common across disciplines and will be highly useful in any environment. The same point applies to teamwork. The conditions in the office may be less extreme and more complex than on the battleground or the sports field. Success on the battleground or the sports field may require a team skill that is narrow and deep, whereas in the office something broader is needed. But the principles behind a successful team are always the same.

The four ingredients for an elite team

There are four essential ingredients to building a great team. Members of an elite team need four abilities:

1. The ability to have faith in each other.
2. The ability to express disagreements with each other in a constructive way.
3. The ability to put the team first, accepting and supporting the team decision even if that is not their choice, and counting success as the success of the team, not of the individuals in it.

4. The ability to hold each other to account if they are falling short.

Patrick Lencioni, in his fabulous book *The Five Dysfunctions of a Team*, looks at this from the other end of the telescope and identifies five problems that weaken a team. I use the word *fabulous* to describe his book deliberately, because three-quarters of it is a realistic fable about a technology company which brilliantly illustrates team dysfunctions and shows how they can be overcome. Lencioni represents the five dysfunctions in a pyramid, as shown in Figure 5.

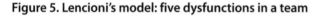

Figure 5. Lencioni's model: five dysfunctions in a team

I prefer to focus on the positive characteristics that a team needs. I represent my ideal team as a circle because of the way in which each characteristic reinforces and interacts with the others – it is a virtuous circle, the opposite of a vicious circle – and because a circle is the perfect shape. I call it the 'Circle of Elite Team Behaviour'– see Figure 6.

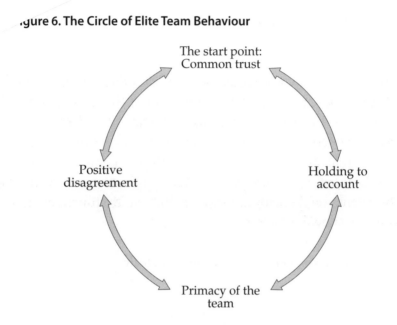

Let me explain in more detail what each point on the circle means.

The start point: common trust

By 'common trust' in a team I mean that its members have faith in one another at an emotional level. They are willing to be authentic with each other and do not have to put on a pretend face to protect themselves. They can just be open with each other about their weaknesses, mistakes, fears and behaviours. And they can do this without feeling vulnerable because they know that, instead of having their frankness exploited by their fellow team members, it will be returned and reciprocated. They reach a point where they can be utterly unguarded with each other and completely open without applying filters. In a team in which proper common trust has been achieved, its members will openly admit their mistakes to each other. They willingly apologise to each other. Because they are able to acknowledge their own weaknesses and each other's strengths, it becomes easy for them to ask each other for help without hesitation when it is needed. A typical feature of a team that has attained common trust is that they can talk about their beliefs and their lives outside work in an easy, friendly way.

Achieving this level of trust in each other is difficult. In many careers we are conditioned to compete with our peer group. Great efforts go into playing political games, designed to make ourselves look good in front of our peers and especially in front of our superiors. It therefore often goes against the grain to fight that conditioning and to show weaknesses, knowledge of which potentially might be used against us in the race to the top of the greasy pole. But if the energy that is burned to further individual agendas inside an organisation can be directed outwards to achieving the organisation's goals, the whole team will benefit.

The team leader has an important role to play in helping to facilitate the achievement of common trust, setting the right culture and making sure that behaviour that leads to mutual faith is rewarded. More on that in the next chapter.

Common trust is the vital start point for elite teamwork.

Positive disagreement

Common trust does not mean that the team always agrees with each other. In fact, quite the reverse. Common trust means that the members of the team can, should and will express the disagreements that they feel. It becomes possible to engage in frank and open debate about the issues that are important to the success of the team and the organisation. Because common trust makes it possible for discussions to be passionate and unguarded, they become compelling, interesting and exciting instead of safe, bland and dull. Team meetings become exciting. Teammates who have really achieved common trust do not hesitate to disagree or to challenge and question one another, all in the spirit of finding the best answers and making good decisions.

If a team does not get to this level, its members will hold back. They will disagree underneath the surface about issues, for sure, but they will not fully express their true opinions. As a result, problems will not be resolved, but will fester, irritate and ultimately poison the team. If issues are not debated face-to-face in meetings, they will be talked about surreptitiously, bitchily, behind people's backs. Then they will become damaging and destructive.

True excellence can only be achieved when team members question each other about how they arrived at their conclusions, and really challenge and test each other. When a disagreement occurs, the team with common trust confronts and deals with the issues before moving on, ensuring that issues are resolved, not ignored. Intellectual rigour leads to robust decision-making, and an effective collective team brain is most likely to deliver intellectual rigour.

For disagreement to be positive, it needs to be respectful. Disagreement about issues should not be allowed to dissolve into personal differences. Discussions should remain at the level of principle and ideas, on an intellectual plane, and should not be dragged down into personal recriminations. If the team enjoys common trust there will be no personal recriminations. But their discussions can and should still be passionate, heated and unrestrained.

Sometimes, a lack of time is used as an excuse not to engage in proper debate about important issues. There can be a perception that meetings which really thrash issues through to a conclusion absorb time that would be better spent on action. In fact, in the medium term, resolving issues properly saves a great deal of time and energy.

It is a bad mistake for attendees at a team meeting to ignore underlying disagreements between other team members which are not expressed. It is far more helpful to bring issues out onto the table so that they can be resolved than to allow them to remain hidden away underneath it. In a team that lacks common trust in each other, an individual who points out differences between colleagues may be seen as a disruptive troublemaker. In a team that is striving for common trust, however, exposing disagreements will be seen as a constructive step on the way to a solution.

The role of the team leader is discussed in more depth in the next chapter, but is in part to close the debate and to confirm the way forward, once the issues have been debated as fully as possible. The team has to be decisive even when perfect information is not available. At that point, the team members must fall in behind the group decision.

Primacy of the team

This is point three on the Circle of Elite Team Behaviour. It involves every team member making the commitment to the common goal and putting that goal first. It means committing to the actions that the team as a whole has decided are necessary to achieve that common goal, whether or not an individual team member supported those actions initially in the debate. And it means measuring success by the team's achievements of those goals, not by the performance of individual team members. After a team that genuinely trusts each other has engaged in unfiltered positive disagreement, it should be easier for everyone to support important decisions, even if individual views were initially at odds. This is because all the options have been put on the table and considered. Everyone has had their say. Everyone's views have been respectfully considered by the rest of the group. Team members leave these meetings clear about the decisions that were taken, and confident that everyone is committed to following them through.

Consensus is sometimes taken as commitment, but in fact is one of its greatest enemies. It is rare that a consensus decision is the correct one; more often it will be a decision which pleases nobody because it is a compromise for everyone. In a team that has common trust, each member will be able to unite behind a decision even if they do not fully agree with it. If a proper debate has been held, and every view listened to and considered, it becomes easier to commit to the agreed direction, even if it is not everyone's first choice.

The desire for certainty can also be an obstruction to decisions and commitment. Often it is not possible to be absolutely sure that a particular decision is right. Sometimes a full set of data is not available, and assumptions have to be made. Most decisions are forward-looking, and the crystal ball that can clearly predict the future simply does not exist. Elite teams understand that it is better to take a clear decision and to stick to it, rather than to fail to take a decision in the hope that it becomes easier at the next meeting. If the decision that is taken is subsequently shown to be wrong, an elite team will be able to change direction without recriminations.

If an executive team fails to commit to a collective decision, ambiguity and uncertainty will permeate the organisation. Small gaps between the team members at the top of an organisation are likely to become chasms between departments lower down, with very damaging results.

The 'primacy of the team' also means that the attention of its members will be focused on team results, not individual results. When the team fails to achieve collective goals, each member must take personal responsibility for improving team performance, whether or not that individual member has been personally responsible for contributing to the miss or not. Team members should willingly make sacrifices in their own areas for the good of the team, and not worry about seeking credit for their own contributions. A corollary of this is that members of such a team will place little importance on titles and status.

A team that can achieve this behaviour is likely consistently to attain its objectives. Teams that commit to this behaviour will set aside their individual needs and agendas and focus on what is best for the team. They do not give in to the temptation to place their departments, career aspirations or ego-driven status ahead of the collective results that define team success. As a result, each individual in the team will benefit and achieve things that they could not hope for on their own.

Holding to account

Step four is 'holding to account'. Strong teams that commit to firm decisions and to high standards of performance will not hesitate to hold one another accountable for adhering to those standards and sticking to those decisions. What is equally important is that they do not rely on the leader as the sole, or even primary, source of accountability. They go directly to their peers. In an elite team, members call out each other's behaviour if it falls short of the required standards. In particular, elite team members will quickly and frankly confront peers about problems in the area for which they have specific responsibility. In this way, the team itself ensures that poor performance is not accepted.

In a properly functioning team, this feedback can be extremely rapid because it can be offered when it is still unproven. Taken in the correct spirit, feedback can itself be debated frankly in the same way that the original decision was reached. It is essential for team members to be able to point out to each other which aspects of what they each do are good, and which are bad.

Sometimes team members feel uncomfortable holding their peers to account. They believe that dealing with poor performance is the prerogative of the team leader, and may worry that addressing it themselves will damage their personal relationships with their colleagues. In fact, the opposite is more often the case. If you see that your friend is not performing or doing what has been agreed, you are likely to become irritated with them. Failing to speak out will just allow that irritation to fester, spoiling the relationship on your side far more than a frank conversation between two team members who have faith in one another and do not want to let each other down. You will also be doing your teammate a disservice because if their poor performance continues it will have a negative impact on them – either as a result of the team performance suffering or because the team leader needs to become involved in sorting out the problem.

Holding each other to account is a large step towards minding more about team results than your own individual results. Just as team members should hold their colleagues to account, they should be quick to point to one another's successes. This helps them to value collective success more than individual success.

Elite teams in practice

If you think that this sounds like idealistic eyewash, take care to listen to the post-match interviews given by the members of the next great sports team to triumph at a major tournament or to win a major title. The language of each and every one of them will be the language of the Circle of Elite Team Behaviour. They will be talking not primarily about their own performance, but about the performance of the team. When the interviewer asks a player such as Fernando Torres if he was pleased to score a goal, he will answer along the lines of, 'Yes, of course, but what really matters is that we won the match. It was the team's performance that made the difference. Xavi's pass to me for the goal was brilliant. Iker Casillas made some fantastic saves. The back four were rock solid. Our midfield worked their socks off, chasing down every ball and dominating the middle of the park.'

And if you think that Torres responds like that because he oozes personal modesty, you need to take a reality check. He responds like that because he understands what you need in an elite team. The same can be said for Team Sky when they won the 2012 Tour de France with Bradley Wiggins.

Team talk

I recently worked with an international sports team that was struggling to achieve its full potential. We talked about the four points on the Circle of Elite Team Behaviour. Heads were nodding in agreement; they'd all heard most of the principles before from other coaches, even if expressed in slightly different ways. I decided to test them out.

'Great,' I said. 'I can see that you really understand this stuff. Let's move on and just check out how you think you are doing in practical terms. Let's start with accountability. How good do you think you are at that? I want you each to write down on a separate piece of paper the score out of ten that you'd give the team on your ability to hold each other to account for each other's performance.'

They wrote down their marks, I collected the pieces of paper, and the average worked out at eight out of ten.

'Okay,' I said, 'you reckon you're pretty good at this. I want to do a morale-building exercise. So sit down in a circle. Now I want each of you in turn – starting with the captain – to take the hot seat and for the rest of you to identify his strengths and what he needs to continue doing.'

The noise rose in the room as they fell over each other to outline each other's strengths.

'Right. Thank you. Now do the same thing but tell your teammates what they are not good at. What do they need to improve? Even more important, tell each other what you need to stop doing because it's holding the team back.'

Absolute silence fell in the room as the penny dropped and they realised that 'holding to account' means supporting your colleagues but most of all telling them if they do not meet an agreed standard of performance.

The lack of willingness to provide constructive criticism to colleagues is one of the major weaknesses in most of the organisations I work with.

Learning to give effective feedback

When I first joined the Paras, I began to realise that you have to buy into the ethos of any group you join and be tested against its standards. In order to earn the ticket to join the group you need to learn about the acceptable level of performance. I learnt my role and responsibilities and came to understand that I needed to perform my job really well to earn the right to move up. Ultimately my disappointment was that I expected colleagues in the Paras to have high standards. Sadly, on occasion, training standards were not met to the degree they should have been. In a team you can influence those around you by doing it right and not cutting corners. As soon as your own standards begin to slip, you will have a negative impact on the other members of the team. *Authenticity* is a word with powerful meaning for me. Authenticity means actually doing what you feel, think and say. If ever I have failed to do that I have had to look in the mirror and acknowledge I have been less than authentic and do something about it.

For a period of time in the Army, after what I saw as numerous experiences of people cutting corners in difficult situations, I could be very hostile with other team members if I felt that standards were not being met. I thought that I was just being forceful, but looking back I can see that people on the receiving end could have seen my approach as dogmatic or autocratic. If I heard people saying, 'Let's do this' and I disagreed with them, I would let them know in a very direct way. I was not always wrong, or always right, but I was normally communicating badly. I had moved through the ranks quite quickly, and I had forgotten to upgrade my communication style. After some incidents like this, a good friend and mentor took me on one side and told me that I was in danger of being sidelined. I was shocked. My ego kicked in, and I remember my defensive and angry outburst: 'What do you mean by that? Why should I lower my standards?' He quietly explained that I was saying things – sometimes the right things – in the wrong way. I listened and took note when he broke the news to me that some officers in the

Regiment were unhappy about working with me. They found me too forthright. My desire to be direct and to press for the right approach at all costs had become too aggressive and counterproductive. My mentor simply said, 'You are being outmanoeuvred; you are not being effective because you are not adapting your game plan.' I paused for a moment and experienced the great sensation of true understanding. I realised how right my friend was, and I was filled with gratitude. He had helped to teach me the need for patience, for careful explanation of what I believed, and the need to listen to others. I learnt the important lesson that going head to head with people does not necessarily get the best results. This awareness of my environment, of other stakeholders and the need to understand their position and adapt to it quickly, was to become essential to my growth as a leader.

Going outside the team

In occasional circumstances, your paramount loyalty to your team may make it necessary to take problems to your team leader, or even to go over their head to a higher authority. Doing so has to be a last resort. You must make sure that you have done everything you can within the team. If you do take an issue outside your team, it can all too easily appear that you are arrogant and 'holier than thou'. If your action is misjudged, it may do damage to the team, and it is likely to do even more damage to yourself. Ultimately you need to be very sure that you are right, but you should have the courage not to shy away from standing firm if wrongdoing needs to be exposed and acted against.

As with the example I have just given, I have found in the past that developing a relationship with someone outside the team who can act as a mentor for you is very worthwhile. It is very valuable to be able to use someone impartial as a sounding board and an advisor before taking potentially irrevocable action which may be harmful if you are wrong.

Most organisations have processes in place that enable individuals to take issues to a level of seniority outside their team, and it is clearly important that, if you decide on this action, you follow those processes. You will be surprised how often the senior people may have inklings about the issues you bring to them.

Personalities in a team

Chapter Two, I hope, put some science behind what we all know: that everyone is different. This is important to remember when working in a team. Do not let the similarities – of personality, culture or objective – obscure the differences, and remember that you will need to compromise and adapt your behaviour towards your teammates if you are to be an effective team member and to avoid being a disruptive influence.

Interesting work has been done by Rose Macauley on how various combinations of personality types affect team dynamics. If a team is composed largely of individuals of similar personality types, its members will naturally come to understand each other more quickly than if the component types are different. So groups with very similar members are likely to reach decisions more quickly. However, this does not mean that they will take good decisions. In fact, they will probably make more errors because fewer viewpoints will be represented. On the other hand, groups made up of many different types will reach decisions more slowly. And the process of reaching a decision is likely to be painful, but the outcome may be better simply because more viewpoints are taken into account during the process. More possibilities are considered, more eventualities are discussed and a fuller range of external reactions to the team's plan are taken into account – because that range of external reactions will vary depending on the personality type of the reactor.

Team balance
Of course, there is a balance to be achieved here. Team members

who are opposite on all four preferences (ISTJ versus ENFP or ESFJ versus INTP, for example) may have trouble achieving full mutual understanding. Members who share two preferences from each of the opposites may be necessary to act as translators between the diametric opposites. It is a little like those word-ladder puzzles where you have to turn one four-letter word into another in a certain number of moves by changing one letter each time:

TEAM	ISTJ
TEAS	ISTP
TENS	ISFP
TINS	INFP
WINS	ENFP

Team members who learn to appreciate and work with different types may help to defuse conflict, and these conciliators may often be 'Feeling' types with a stronger natural desire for harmony and 'teamness' than the 'Thinking' types with their focus on hard facts, truth and task.

Out on your own

It can be especially difficult if one individual is the only representative of a certain preference in the whole team because they may be seen as an oddball with different views or behaviour from all the others, which therefore do not have validity. Extroverts may dominate discussions in a team and thus perhaps decision-making, unless they make a special effort to involve the introverts; those introverts may need to make a special effort to be heard and to be more vociferous than they feel comfortable being, in order to have an impact.

One-sided teams

It is possible for teams to succeed if they are 'one-sided', with few types, but they will greatly enhance their chances of success if they use balancing characteristics from outside the team as a resource, or if they make a determined and conscious effort to use their own less preferred characteristics as the tasks require. Team members will usually choose tasks that fit the gifts of their type.

Multi-type teams
The best teams are likely to comprise a range of types. The best decisions are likely to be reached when:

1. The basic facts and realities have been taken into account (requiring 'Sensing' skills).
2. Useful new possibilities have been opened up (requiring an 'iNtuitive' approach).
3. Consistencies and inconsistencies have been analysed ('Thinking').
4. Important values have been considered ('Feeling').

What is more, in these successful, multi-type teams, significant personal development is likely to take place, further strengthening the team, as learning will result from an understanding of the opposite gifts of the others. In these teams, the leadership roles may shift as the tasks to be done require different types of skill, enhancing the team's harmony and sense of balance.

Of course, a good leader has a vital role to play in unlocking the team's full potential, ensuring harmonious working and drawing out particular characteristics and skills when they are most needed. More on that in the next chapter.

So what?

Human beings have grouped together in teams ever since they evolved because in that way the individuals in the team can achieve more than they can on their own. Of course you cannot win a game of football except as part of a team, but even in 'individual' sports like tennis or athletics, the person on the court or the track is part of a team – the coach, the physio, the fitness specialist and the rest. All businesses, even the smallest, are teams, and most are teams of teams. So functioning as well as possible as part of the team is essential to success.

Everyone wants the trust of their teammates, and you know that you perform best when you enjoy that trust. Thus it follows that if you want your teammates to perform at their best you must show them that same trust. That is the foundation, the starting point for the other elite team characteristics: the power of disagreement in reaching the right decision, the primacy of the team over individual interests, and the ability to hold your teammates to account for their performance and to be held to account in turn.

Your knowledge of the inner workings of the brain (Chapter One), your self-awareness and awareness of other personality types (Chapter Two), your motivation and focus (Chapter Three), and your ability to communicate effectively (Chapter Four) and to perfect your skills through training (Chapter Five) are the individual talents you need to bring to the team. But it is the ability to function as part of a team that provides the framework for those talents to achieve their full potential.

CHAPTER SEVEN

You as a team leader

Leadership is the art of getting someone else to do something
you want done because he wants to do it.

Dwight D. Eisenhower

'Behind enemy lines'

'Meanwhile, Delta Eight had had a successful couple of nights.
They'd destroyed several sections of the communications conduits
down the MSR. On the mission's second night they'd found a
number of planes on a nearby airfield and had called down an air
strike which eliminated the threat in spectacular style. It was now
late afternoon. The weather had been behaving in an unexpected
way; it had been intensely cold, with flurries of sleet and snow, but
they had been ready for that and had not been too uncomfortable
in their waterproof kit and sleeping bags. The camouflage-netted
Pinkies also provided some shelter from the weather. A couple of
the team were cleaning their weapons, checking that there was
no sand or grit in the mechanisms, and another was packing away
equipment in readiness for moving out on the evening operation.
The vehicles were tucked away at the bottom of a wadi, drawn
up at the base of the steepest slope and facing outwards down
the valley, in case a quick getaway was required. Kevin and Mick
were on sentry duty in vantage points above the wadi. Martin had
posted two sentries and they were especially alert because the
patrol's position was far from perfect; there were areas of dead
ground on both sides. Their airfield foray and the process of calling

in the strike had held them up and this was just the best location that they could find in the hour before dawn. The risk of moving in the light would have been greater than staying in their imperfect situation. They knew that their sabotage activity, and especially the destruction of the planes, would alert the enemy to the likely presence of a Special Forces group in the area, but they had to hope that their tracks had not been picked up and that, if any enemy troops did spot them, their knowledge of the vicinity was no better than theirs.

'That hope was shattered by the call "Stand to, stand to" sounding from Kevin. His tone was calm, but urgent. "Two enemy vehicles approaching from the north-west. One jeep fitted with a 7.62 MG-34 machine gun. One covered truck." They all knew that the covered truck could mean eighteen, maybe twenty enemy soldiers.

'Instantly activity began at pace. It was silent, controlled, but rapid. They packed away the last of their equipment into the Pinkies. As you know by now, we never take off our belt kit, and we always have our weapons beside us, so all they had to do was reach out and grab them. They moved impassively to the pre-arranged positions that had been allocated the night before, communicating silently with hand signals. They were following drills that they had rehearsed many times before. Everyone shared a calm intensity.

'Then, from behind them, to the east, rattled a volley of automatic fire. Making use of the dead ground, another large attacking force had gathered at the top of the hill on the opposite side of the valley. They were three hundred, three hundred and twenty yards away. They looked well disciplined and must have outnumbered Delta Eight at least two, maybe three, to one. The group in the vehicles had been a diversion, but now also presented the real danger of blocking the patrol's exit from the wadi.

'Even worse, on the very first volley Delta Eight had a wounded man. Martin was down, hit in the back. He looked badly hurt. Tom, as corporal, had to assume command. The team was already holding to its defensive position. Tom saw with satisfaction that every man was working to a game plan that had been practised many times. Each man knew his role. The patrol medic – Wings – was getting a field dressing on Martin's wound and administering morphine.

'Tom gave brief commands to establish exactly what the enemy position was and deliver fire-control orders. The trust the team had built up meant that no one wasted time looking to see what the others were doing. They only had to concentrate on their own job. They needed to establish a foundation and win the fire fight against their numerically much stronger enemy.

'Briefly Tom took himself out of the battle so that he could plan the appropriate course of action. The concentration of accurate firepower and unity was now having the desired effect on the enemy. Delta Eight was beginning to gain the upper hand. But Tom could see that they would have to get out of the valley quickly before the other enemy group could come around and block them in.

'"Move out! Now! Into the vehicles!" Tom's voice echoed over the gunfire around the walls of the wadi, and his meaning was reinforced by his hand signals. He turned to help Wings lift Martin into the nearest Pinkie. Less than a minute later the two Land Rovers were underway, accelerating furiously down the slope. As soon as they were clear of the wadi, they were able to open up with their vehicle-mounted Brens, which dramatically increased the patrol's firepower. From the front vehicle, Colin raked the ridge occupied by the enemy squad whose volley had wounded Martin. From the second Land Rover, Mick concentrated his fire on the enemy jeep, whose mounted machine gun posed the greatest threat, although the rounds it was firing were flying well wide. Firing a machine gun accurately over two, three hundred yards from a vehicle lurching over rough ground is no easy task, but it is a skill that we practise over and over again. Mick's training paid off when the jeep suddenly lurched to the right, hit a boulder and turned over. Without hesitating, Mick moved his fire onto the covered truck. Even at that distance they could see bits flying off it, and it ground to a halt.

'"Wings, how's Martin doing?"

Wings looked over into the back seat where Martin was slumped, ashen-faced under his beard and unconscious.

'"Not good; not good at all. We need to get him out."

'"Right. We'll head for the emergency pick-up point blue and call in a plane to evacuate him. That'll also make some distance between us and the hostiles. You okay with that?"

'Wings and Colin nodded their assent. Tom beckoned the second Pinkie to catch them up and outlined the plan in a few words. The rest of the team quickly gave their buy-in and they all settled into the drive. The allied control of the air meant that there would be no threat from that direction, and the welcome blanket of night was now falling fast. As they bounced over the desert, Wings continued to provide first aid to Martin and Colin called in the plane.

'Six hours later, around midnight, Delta Eight reached the rendezvous point. The jolting ride had not been good for Martin, who moved in and out of semi-consciousness. Wings did everything he could to keep him stable, checking that the bleeding from the wound was under control and administering occasional top-up doses of morphine. But they did not know whether he was going to live or die.

'At the rendezvous they killed their engines and waited in silence for a couple of minutes, listening intently for sounds of pursuit. They heard nothing except the wind. But Tom was taking no chances.

'"Right. Steve, take the Pinkie back a couple of hundred yards the way we came and cover our tracks. Get a couple of men up on that higher ground to either side. The plane should be here in thirty."

'Sure enough, half an hour later a faint rumble to the south indicated a distant aircraft. The noise grew into a roar, and then into the distinctive rush of air as the plane landed on the short strip of land. It came to rest and spun around. Tom and Wings carried Martin over and delivered him into the care of the waiting medical team, who immediately began to check his vital signs and hook him up to a drip. Then came the surprise.

'The captain who had delivered the original briefing appeared in the doorway.

'"Tom? You are in charge now?" He handed over a headset so that they could hear each other properly over the din of the still spinning propellers. The engines of course continued running so as to waste no time in lifting back off again.

'"There is another patrol out here. Delta Nine. They don't have vehicles. We picked up a signal from them early this morning. We don't know their status; all we had was the emergency signal. We assume they had a contact and something's gone wrong. Their wireless must be disabled, or they would not have used the emergency comms to contact us. Their last known position is seventy kilometres west of here. Find them if you can and get them out. Here's what you need." The captain passed over a brown envelope and patted Tom on the shoulder. "Good hunting."'

†

Moving from team membership to leadership

In an elite team the move from team membership to team leadership should be a natural progression. In a fully functioning team, the responsibilities of membership vary relatively little from the responsibilities of leadership. Just as members in an elite team move into leadership in certain circumstances, or into leadership of certain tasks, so the elite team leader will never lose sight of what it is like to be a member of the team. If the members of the team are successfully interacting with each other, contributing to each other's motivation, providing effective positive criticism and feedback, the tactical day-to-day elements of the team leader's role in particular become far easier. The leader is able to focus more energy outwards at strategic objectives, to the benefit of the team overall.

The principles of team leadership

If the ideal team leader is only a small step away from being a team member, then it follows that the way the leader should behave is similar to the way in which a team member should behave. The first step is for the leader to demonstrate the same common trust that they wish the members of the team to display. The strong team leader will not shelter behind their position and status, but will show the same openness and vulnerability expected of the members of the team. Rather than imposing authority from above, the team leader should admit to mistakes and weaknesses, apologise where necessary, seek help in a non-authoritarian way and communicate with team members in the same open, friendly manner in which they are expected to communicate with each other. Showing the team how to behave by example is essential.

Few things are more powerful than a team leader telling the team how they got to be a leader. When I work with a leader I ask them to outline a simple timeline of their career to their team and to explain its key elements. I ask them to talk about what they bring to the leadership role, what the role gives to them, which parts of the role they find most difficult and what support they need. This often turns out to be one of the most effective ten-minute communications they will ever make. In every case where I have carried out this exercise you could have heard a pin drop. The audience is riveted because the leader is exposing themself and demonstrating the faith and trust that they want the team to show to each other. It is unusual for a leader to reveal their weaknesses to their junior colleagues or reports. Far from demonstrating weakness, to do so shows great strength. It is a sign of elite leadership.

LEADERSHIP MEANS CONNECTING

It is not a perfect world

Of course, in practice life is not that simple and leading by example is not always enough on its own. Problems will occur even in the best teams from time to time, and at least initially most team leaders are faced with imperfect teams for whom example will not be enough. Often bad behavioural habits need to be changed quickly, and team dynamics improved. Teams generally need nurture, inspiration and motivation to reach the levels of performance at which the leader's own efforts can be safely turned outwards. But the leader also needs to make the individuals in the team realise that there are consequences for not conforming to the right behaviour that can eventually lead to dismissal.

What to do when you take on leadership of a team

The first thing to do is to understand the group dynamics and to help the group to understand those dynamics themselves. If I take on the leadership of a team, or the responsibility for mentoring a team, I like first of all to get the team members' views on how the team is working. To do so I ask the team to answer a simple questionnaire covering team behaviour:

1. Are team meetings interesting, not dull?
2. Will team members apologise to each other if they do something that might damage the team?
3. During team meetings, are the most controversial issues discussed and resolved?
4. At the end of team discussions, are decisions made to which all team members commit?
5. Do team members leave meetings confident that their colleagues will fulfil these commitments?
6. If a team member thinks a colleague is doing something wrong, do they tell them?
7. Are issues debated openly between team members and with passion?
8. Do team members know about each other's personal lives and discuss them happily with each other?
9. Will team members readily sacrifice budget or resources in their own area for the good of the team?
10. Do team members really hate the idea of letting down their colleagues?
11. Do team members acknowledge their own weaknesses to each other?
12. Do the team challenge one another about their plans and how they carry them out?

I ask each team member to answer each question with a score ranging from 1 to 5, where 1 indicates a 'strong no' and 5 indicates a 'strong yes'. Clearly there is some crossover between the questions (it is a connected circle, after all), but principally the questions relate to each of the four points on the Circle of Elite Team Behaviour described in Chapter Six as follows:

	Questions
Point 1: Common trust	2, 8, 11
Point 2: Positive disagreement	1, 3, 7
Point 3: Primacy of the team	4, 5, 9
Point 4: Holding to account	6, 10, 12

I add up the scores and allocate them as above so that each point on the circle has a total ranging between 3 and 15. A score of between 3 and 7 means that the team is falling far short of where it should be in that area; between 8 and 11 that some improvement is needed; and between 12 and 15 that the team is doing pretty well and touching elite standards of behaviour.

Of course, individual team members' responses will vary, which may indicate that they are more or less demanding or score more or less strictly, or that they have different perceptions of how the team is performing.

My next step is to talk through the outcome of these questionnaires individually with each team member. In this way I get a good picture of the dynamics in the team, of each individual's role in it and of the way in which they perceive the functioning of the team.

'Reculer pour mieux sauter'
Having digested the outcome of the questionnaire and learnt as much as possible about the team's own perceptions of how things are working, I like to take time out to run through various exercises with the team. Especially if the team has been performing poorly and is under pressure, they will often resist sparing the time and want to rush on to training or action. However, until any problematic issues in the team have been resolved, rushing forward is likely to be a waste of time. It will further entrench

problems and will be far less productive than it could be. It may even be counterproductive. This really is a case of *'reculer pour mieux sauter'* ('to draw back in order to make a better jump'). A few steps back and a good run-up mean that you can jump a lot further than from a stationary standing position. As I said in Chapter Five, advanced training is about doing the basics really well. Moving on before you have got the basics right undermines the whole process. Team management is just the same – you have to get the basics right before you can safely move on.

It is worth taking some time away from the normal workplace to explain your vision for the team and the way that you wish it to function, and then to run through the following exercises.

Personality mix

The first exercise is to consider the group's personality types. Even if some or all of the team have carried out some form of personality profiling in the past, they should do so again and share the results with each other. The team leader should act as moderator, explaining the significance of different personality types, and being especially careful to emphasise that no particular type is inherently better or worse than any other. Most people are intrigued by definitions of personality types because of the light that they can cast on themselves and others. Talking about types as a group and relating them to individuals' real-life behaviour can in itself begin to break down barriers and start the process of enabling team members to understand each other better.

Then the team needs to consider what conclusions can be drawn from the group's personality mix. You should ask what are the strengths and potential weaknesses about the mix? Is your team a homogenous group which is likely to need external input to reach the best decisions (as described in Chapter Six)? If so, how do you set about getting that external input? Or is the team composed of disparate types between which communications may need to be carefully managed to be effective? Is the team missing any important characteristics? Are any additional features needed to make it stronger? Is there anything that prevents the team from being better than it is?

Of course, considering the personality profiles of the team, and the mix of those profiles, at the start of your team-building process is not only useful for the team members, it will also add to your knowledge as team leader about how best to communicate with each individual yourself.

I remember once working with a group of fourteen who were responsible for innovation in their company. When we ran through personality profiles for the group we discovered that thirteen of the team were very low on the iNtuitive characteristic. The team was far too biased towards Sensing types. We immediately realised that other members would have to be brought into the team when creative rather than scientific solutions were required.

Personal history

In many teams, it is surprising how little members may know about each other even if they have worked together for some time. A very simple but effective exercise is to ask each team member to name five things, important to them, that they would like other team members to know. This might include naming family members, outlining past achievements of which they are proud, listing hobbies, summarising beliefs or mentioning a few favourite things. Some of these will be a revelation to the others sitting round the table and may provide a fresh point of communication, something new to talk about. The exercise highlights that everyone in the team is a real person, not just a work colleague, and will help to personalise team relationships.

I recently carried out a variant of this exercise with a group that was working together for the first time. Their initial meeting had been tense and they had been reluctant to move forward on a number of issues. In the evening I asked them each to sketch a simple timeline starting from the age of sixteen and to tell the others how they had reached their current positions. They could use anything to help tell their story. Some members of the team really gave a good account of their journey, which provided some interesting insights. The next day they all had much more patience with one another and were willing to listen. By the end of the conference they had made decisions and committed to them.

Perceptions of strengths and weaknesses

Follow on from this exercise, which should have generated some banter and laughter and relaxed the atmosphere, to something that is higher-risk because it has the potential to provoke conflict. Ask everyone in the team to jot down the main strength that each other team member brings, and then one weakness or type of behaviour that they need to improve or eliminate for the greater good. Focusing on each team member one by one, go round the table asking each individual to read out what they have written. Start by soliciting your team's views about yourself. During this exercise do not debate these perceptions; the objective is just to identify and acknowledge them.

This exercise may uncover some positive or negative behaviours about which the person being critiqued was unaware, at least consciously. More likely, it will confirm things which were already known to be issues, but which had not been fully explored or discussed in an open way. Recognising positives first and demonstrating how they are appreciated and valued by others around the table creates a receptive atmosphere for exposing weaknesses. Bringing undesirable behaviours out into the light when they have previously been allowed to stew in the dark can be a very cathartic moment and can start the process of addressing and eliminating the behaviour that irritates and weakens the team.

Rules of engagement for constructive disagreement

This last exercise in itself may help you draw some conclusions about the degree of frankness that the team will be able to achieve immediately in debate. Discuss with the team the rules of engagement for interaction and discussion. The objective is to achieve absolutely frank and open communication, but ground rules need to be set for how this takes place. What should be the methods of communicating with one another? Are particular conduits damaging relationships? For example, are emails – perhaps too terse or too wordy for individual tastes, too widely or too narrowly circulated, or copied to certain recipients for political point-scoring reasons – causing friction inside the team? Email traffic needs to have rules or you end up with people who appear to think they come to work just to pass on emails to one another. Would an old-fashioned face-to-face conversation (often the most effective form of communication) be a better way of delivering the message, or would a phone call suffice? Get the team to consider and understand the impact that particular types and styles of communication can have on the recipient.

Having talked earlier about personality types, the team should be able to understand better the likely impact of communicating with their peers in particular ways. Extroverts may enjoy the cut and thrust of debate more than Introverts, whose instinct may be to go away and chew over issues by themselves. Sensing types will want more hard facts than the iNtuitive types. Thinking types may be happy with information being delivered in a simple, direct, purely rational way, whereas Feeling types are likely to prefer an approach that empathises more with them. And of course, armed with their personality type self-knowledge, the recipient of the communication should also be able to understand better why a particular form of delivery feels better or worse, and therefore to control more effectively their own emotional reaction to it. As someone with a tendency towards Feeling, when I was younger, if I listened to a person with a Thinking tendency, I would automatically think they were unconcerned about the effect of their message or actions on me and on other people. This was not necessarily the case, but it could also cause me to argue my point more forcefully or be dismissive of the message or action. Now I know that it is just the way they put their message across and that it is the way that I receive it that needs to be adapted.

If the structure of the organisation requires it, you should also discuss how interaction should take place with each other's staff. For example, are there any circumstances in which it is acceptable for one team member to go straight to another's direct report? If the management structure is more matrix-style, how should the additional complications be handled? How should shared resources be allocated and used? How should priorities be determined? How important are meetings and how much time should they take? It often surprises me that meetings in many of the organisations that I visit conclude without actions at the end or indeed lack any checks to see if they are on track. On other occasions I have seen too many checks imposed with the result that there is no time to get anything done as everyone is constantly updating information instead of doing their job. The old 80/20 rule also works here: 80 per cent action and 20 per cent quality discussion and decision-making is the right mix. The precise points to discuss will vary from organisation to organisation, according to their size, structure and purpose. But the objective is to establish and agree clear ground rules to which all team members can commit. Yes, 'commit' – that word again.

It is also worth drawing on the first exercise and considering whether there is anything in the mix of personality types that will make it difficult to engage in positive disagreement. There may also be some experiences in the group that make it harder for certain members to engage in positive disagreement. The mix of personalities will determine what style of disagreement is acceptable to the group. It always needs to be respectful and based on principles not personalities, but how forceful can it be?

The objective must always be to move as rapidly as possible to a position whereby the team can express disagreement with each other in a positive, open and passionate way. Your role as team leader is to help the team to understand why disagreement is productive. It will save time in the medium term and will engender efficiency. Explain to your team that, by avoiding disagreement in meetings or face-to-face conversations with colleagues, far from avoiding hurting their feelings they are storing up future problems; if an issue is not resolved openly it will lead to damaging discord behind people's backs, and duplicitous political behaviours that are far more harmful than a vigorous debate. Far from showing respect, a refusal to say what you think in disagreement with a colleague shows disrespect because it implies that you think they are too weak to cope with your dissenting view. You do not hold them in high enough regard to say what you really think. Remind the team that the right kind of forceful disagreement means respect, not disrespect.

Releasing tension inside the team

One useful technique for releasing tension in the team is to dig out disagreements. Some team members may naturally fulfil this role (typically those with 'Thinking' and 'Judging' characteristics). If you do not have any of these 'conflict miners' in your team, you may need to perform this function regularly yourself, and highlight areas of disagreement between team members so that they can be discussed and resolved.

If your team appears to be backing away from positive disagreement, you may need to repeat the message that disagreement is productive and desirable, and that your team has freely accepted that it is acceptable behaviour, subject to the agreed rules of engagement. Reinforcing the message that openly disagreeing with a colleague is far more respectful than refusing to voice your disagreement can be a useful way to reduce tension if a debate is becoming too heated. Remind your team that the purpose of discussion is to find solutions, not just to raise problems.

However, as a team leader you need to avoid becoming overprotective of your reports. This can be a natural tendency for team leaders. But if you close off discussions before they have been resolved, the benefit of positive disagreement will not be realised. Your team's development will be hindered, not helped, and they will not develop the skills that they need to cope effectively with debate. So do not allow your natural tendency to want to 'protect' the people who report to you – even if only from each other – to become an obstacle to good team leadership.

Reaching commitment

As team leader one of your most important roles is to steer your team towards decisions so that they can then commit to them. This emphatically does not mean imposing your own view on the group. Indeed, to do so would undermine much of the work that you have done so far to create a fully functioning team, by forcing your colleagues back into their shells and endangering the open, vulnerable communication that you are trying to foster. However, once an issue has been debated fully, and all disagreements constructively aired, it is your role to pull the threads together and to express what the team has decided. Remember always to use the word *we* when you are expressing the conclusion: 'So, to summarise, I think we have agreed that we should …' not 'I have heard what you all have to say, and my decision is to …'.

An essential part of the decision, and the team's ability to commit to it, is the deadline by which it should be fulfilled. As leader, you need to make sure that timescales and schedules are part of the discussion that takes place. It is always helpful for clear notes of a meeting to be taken for circulation shortly afterwards to all the participants. However brief these notes are, the most important element is a timeline of crystal clarity. Teams that find commitment difficult are often plagued by ambiguity; a date is an absolute fact about which there can be no wooliness, so a clear schedule is a useful tool in the drive towards clarity. It is also important to make one person responsible for the outcome of each action. Of course they may draw on support and resources from others, but it is vital that only one person is ultimately responsible.

Once you have articulated the key decisions that have been taken, it is a useful technique at the end of any meeting to discuss how those decisions should be communicated. The communication required may be internal within the organisation, upwards, downwards or sideways. Or it may be external, to customers, suppliers, shareholders or other constituencies. Whomever the communication is for, the process of resolving how the decisions should be disseminated can often flush out residual disagreements or misunderstandings about what has been agreed. Talking explicitly about communication will also highlight whether anything should not be said and instead remain confidential. It should also mean that everyone leaves the meeting genuinely bearing the same message, thus presenting a powerful impression of unity to the outside world. Remember that small nuances of opinion in a team will be amplified as they pass through an organisation, so that something that perhaps did not seem to matter very much in the meeting really can matter further down the line.

Information flows

A short while back I worked with an eight-strong leadership team in a division of a large communications company. This highly-talented team was responsible for the delivery of multi-million-pound key performance indicators (KPIs). In many cases they were each saying exactly the same things but were nevertheless in violent disagreement with each other. It was clear that they lacked common trust and did not understand the primacy of the team. We worked together over a period of three months looking at their working practices and beginning to build that vital element of trust. I applied the principles and techniques set out in this chapter, initially looking at their personality types and assessing how close they were to the four points on the Circle of Elite Team Behaviour. I interviewed each individual one by one. I asked what was going well in the team and what was going badly. I probed to discover who were the most significant people in the team and why. I pressed them to define their view of team success, of the opportunities and the key deliverables in the next six months. It became clear from these conversations that the team was falling short on a number of points:

- They were not treating the leadership team as their number one team, but their own departmental teams instead.
- They had a number of unspoken personal agendas which both caused and fed off their lack of common trust.
- They felt that they were overloaded with work and grappling with impossible targets but were unwilling to discuss with each other how to change this situation.
- They lacked confidence and as a result had become reactive rather than proactive.

Once all these issues and their perceptions of them were brought into the open, the team identified five key goals for the following two months:

- to define a realistic vision for the organisation
- to articulate the reasons why they wanted this vision to succeed
- to create symbols to represent their vision
- to list the key actions to achieve their vision
- to quantify the support they would need to complete those actions.

In the course of discussing each member of the leadership team's mutual needs, it became apparent that the three senior people expected more information from each other than they were getting. Without it, they felt that they were each being marginalised by the others. As soon as this simple point became clear, it brought the explanation from each of them that they felt they were doing the others a favour by not informing them of their problems. They realised immediately what was required. This team went on to great things and within six months each of them was promoted.

If your team finds it difficult to reach conclusions, focus them initially on decisions that are either relatively easy or low risk if they turn out to be wrong. Most groups find making clear decisions habit-forming, not least because a decision channels and releases energy even if future events demonstrate that it is not completely right. Getting used to taking easy decisions is good practice for the hard ones. Another method of nudging an indecisive team in the right direction is to discuss contingency plans. Generally, doing so will demonstrate that even a poor decision is survivable and will not result in the degree of damage that nervous team members may fear.

Most decisions have to be taken based on incomplete information. All decisions deal with the future. You are aiming to resolve what you do next; there is no point in taking a decision about what you have already done. The future is, of course, always unpredictable, because it does not exist yet (unless you are fortunate or unfortunate enough to be some sort of Time Lord). Often, you as leader have to be more willing to accept the risk of a wrong decision than your team. This is in spite of the fact that you as leader will also have to carry the can for the decision. That is your responsibility as the leader.

The ability to understand and accept the dangers or possible dangers ahead are a key aspect of leadership and decision-making. As team leader, you need to visualise the necessary contingencies and prepare the team to deal with them. It is also important to remember that sometimes as a leader you may have to disagree with your entire team and take them in a different direction from the one they choose. Although this situation is rare, as a leader you must be prepared to stand by your own convictions.

When I am faced with a decision, I make an assessment of whether it is low, medium or high risk. I then look at the potential payback on the decision and determine whether that will deliver a low, medium or high return. If you have all the facts, in most cases a decision is easy, but in practice you never do have all the facts. So I make an assessment of whether I am prepared to take the decision based on 50 per cent of the facts or whether I need a greater level of certainty – 60, 70 or 80 per cent. Then I consider what contingency plans I require, especially if high risks are attached. I will always go ahead if my data is 80 per cent complete. I will run with a lower degree of certainty if the risks associated with getting it wrong are low, or if the potential payback is high enough to result in a favourable risk–reward ratio. Especially with a good team around me, I can be reasonably confident that if the decision turns out to be wrong, we can recover from it.

Holding to account

One of the risks of 'strong' leadership is that it can reduce the accountability between team members. If the leader becomes the only source of discipline and the only person who holds the rest of the team to account, the Circle of Elite Team Behaviour can break. Team members will retreat back to their individual silos, focus on building their individual empires and even begin to take pleasure when one of their rivals falls short and 'gets into trouble with the boss'.

So the truly strong team leader must delegate as much as possible of the process of holding team members to account to the co-members of the team. The first step here is to ensure that everyone is aware not just of their own objectives but of their teammates' objectives as well. Publishing the team schedule and team goals is the essential first step towards this end.

Simple though it may seem, the second step is to hold regular progress review meetings with the whole team. Once again, these meetings should not be dominated by the leader holding all the others to account. Individual team members should be encouraged to explain where they are in relation to their goals and to hold themselves to account. If they are falling short but do not recognise it, their peers should be the first to point this out, holding each other to account. Team members who are struggling should be encouraged to ask for help from the others; as a task progresses, aspects of it may turn out to be more complex than originally thought, and may require more resources. This support should be volunteered and willingly given. I've often worked with groups who are happy to pass the responsibility for important decisions upwards to their senior leadership. Even if in their heart of hearts these groups know what a decision should be, they may seek to avoid taking it so that they do not have to face their colleagues. It is essential to stop this behaviour immediately by ensuring that every possible decision is passed to them and that they take ownership for the outcome and consequences. Once you have group accountability, the performance level of a team automatically improves.

If rewards are moved away from individual performance to team performance, a greater culture of accountability is likely to develop. Then everyone is in it together and if the other members of the team see one of their group performing badly, they are unlikely to let it slip by. The fear of letting down teammates, or to put it positively, the desire to perform well for the others, needs to become the prime motivation in an elite team.

Often group tasks are interlinked: 'If you do not do what you are supposed to in time, I will not be able to do what I have to either.' This can lead to a culture of blame where one individual uses the fault of another as an excuse for their own shortfall. The leader must make it clear that this blame game is unacceptable.

Taming any negative voices in the team is also important. There is nothing wrong with people pointing out the dangers of a particular decision; indeed, this is an important part of positive disagreement and of the process of reaching a good decision. However, a constant and persistent negative voice can be extremely damaging to the effectiveness of the team. It also implies that the negative voice has not been able to commit to the team decision and is not putting the interests of the team first. As leader, you have to make it clear to these people that if they are unable to adapt their behaviour, they will not remain in the team for long.

Another form of behaviour that is unacceptable and which the team leader must not permit is the use of 'I told you so'. If these four words appear in the way team members hold each other to account, it implies that their speaker did not properly or genuinely make the commitment to the group decision. The response to these words must be: 'You bought into the decision – you are part of the team and share equal responsibility for it.'

And, ultimately, the leader does have to take responsibility for holding team members to account. They have to be the ultimate arbiter of performance if something goes wrong. Delegating responsibility to the peer group for holding each other to account does not mean that the team leader can totally abdicate that responsibility. If they do, team performance will be determined by consensus and will fall back into a wallow of mediocrity.

One thing that the leader must never do, however, is to blame the team or complain about its members. You are responsible for the team. Its failings are your failings, and if anyone is at fault for them it is you.

An uphill downhill

When I was in the Regiment, one of the skills I mastered was skiing, so as to be ready for mountain warfare. Of course, this was not skiing on nice smooth pistes, but learning how to cover every type of terrain – uphill, downhill, glaciers, snow-free rocks, the works – and how to survive in arctic conditions. In fact, my style on a standard ski slope leaves quite a lot to be desired because I tend to point downhill and just go!

On one occasion I was in charge of a training exercise for novice skiers in the Canadian Rockies. At this stage I'd made the rank of sergeant major and I had three other non-commissioned officers (NCOs) working with me. I asked this team to reconnoitre a route march for the trainees.

The Rockies are one of the most spectacular mountain ranges I have ever seen. In geological terms they are young, and so rough and jagged as to make the Alps look like foothills. The three NCOs were probably the best skiers I have ever come across. They were dropped off by helicopter and took two days to map out a route of 120 kilometres that the novice skiers were expected to cover over three days. Meanwhile I oversaw various other aspects of the training programme.

The recce party got back to base looking completely knackered but grinning all over their faces. 'The beginners are going to love this, Floyd. Let me show you what we've got.' I was infected by their enthusiasm and grinned back, but when they showed me the route they had selected I became very serious very quickly. It involved descending several very narrow couloirs that were not very far off vertical, and two exceptionally long, steep climbs that would take it out of the fittest and most practised individual, let alone novices with no previous experience of climbing on skis. But the worst bit was a traverse along a sharp ridge at 4,100 metres, which offered the prospect of a fatal drop on either side.

'Come off it! You must be joking. Show me the real route.'

'No, Floyd, we're not joking. You know the mantra. Into the pressure zone. Train as if it is for real. This is the sort of thing these guys are going to have to do in real life. The sooner they learn what it's like, the better. I tell you, it's perfectly doable.'

'Well, on the map it looks unbelievably tough to me. But you are the experts and you've checked it out, so I will back your judgement.'

I had taken the wrong decision. The course was far too tough. The novices did complete it, but took a day longer than intended. They had to cope with two white-out storms, staying out for longer than expected in very difficult conditions. They suffered several minor injuries and even more hurt to their pride. I took full responsibility and did not attempt to pass the blame on to anyone else as ultimately I made the call. The debrief that followed enabled the team to express their dismay over my decision. I learnt a number of valuable lessons but most importantly that the leader has to carry the can.

Primacy of the team

The acid test to discover if its members are putting their team first is whether they measure success by the achievement of the team rather than individual goals. As I said in Chapter Six, this behaviour follows on naturally from the process of holding your peers to account, and several of the things you need to do as leader to achieve it are similar.

So, to determine whether you have achieved success or not, you have to define what that success is going to be. Your goals must be specific, measurable and attainable. Everyone in the team must understand precisely what they are, and everyone must believe that they can be reached. So for a sports team, 'being the best in the world' is unlikely to be a sensible team objective. It is woolly and ill-defined (unless it is linked to a very clear sequence of results that determine 'the best in the world'). Realistically, this team objective may also be unattainable. Far better to have as an objective winning a particular tournament or competition, which will present a challenge and stretch the team, but is not so far out of sight as to be unreal.

The process of defining the objectives should, if possible, be a team exercise, to which the whole team commits in the usual way. However, in many organisations the team's discretion about their objectives may be limited. So, for example, sales targets and budgets may be set from on high and the ability of the team or you as team leader to change those may be limited. It may also be the situation that all or some of the remuneration or incentive package is set and cannot be changed. Nevertheless, even where this is the case, it should be possible for the team to set the specific granular targets that have to be achieved in order to meet budgets, and the schedule according to which they need to be achieved. These can then become the goals against which the team measures its group success.

Sometimes, announcing publicly your commitments and goals can be an added incentive to achieve them. In sports teams, this may not make sense because of the way in which it can provoke an opponent. In the corporate arena, where there is no one single opponent, a public commitment can make a team more passionate about achieving that goal. This can be seen in the way that many public companies, whose goals are known to their shareholders and stock market investors, fight harder to achieve their annual results than private companies for whom a missed target is less obvious externally and thus less damaging.

The two main threats preventing team success being the prime objective of its members are connected with status. Status can be damaging in two ways. First, individual status – career prospects, financial reward – can become more important than team results. The team leader must counter this tendency by making sure that peer pressure really matters and is maintained by tailoring wherever possible remuneration to team results, not individual results, and by ensuring that they do not reward behaviour that is driven by individual, not team, concerns.

The second danger of status is perhaps more subtle, and occurs when the reward for the members of the team becomes the status of just being part of that team. It can be very damaging if being a member of a prestigious, even elite, organisation becomes enough on its own. Then, achieving team goals is nice, but not the prime motivation. Just being there is good enough. Of course, if this culture becomes prevalent, the performance and reputation of the organisation concerned will decline and the 'static status' incentive for team members will begin to wither.

To their team, the leader must be focused and driven about achieving results to meet targets. Any suggestion that the team leader is wavering from hitting the target or the deadline gives the team members the excuse to relax and do the same. If your team says, 'We'll do our best' in response to their objectives, it probably means that they are preparing to fall short of their targets. If you say, 'I'll do my best' or 'I'll do what I can' to your team, it gives the same signal.

Dealing with inadequate team members

Because the elite team leader has to take responsibility for their team's result, and can have no excuse for their team's underachievement, it means that you must deal with inadequate team behaviours promptly and decisively. The whole point of this chapter is to equip you with the right understanding to take your team to elite levels. However, it is inevitable, if you inherit a team or even if you build one, that some of its members may not be able to adapt their behaviour in the way that is required to achieve the Circle of Elite Team Behaviour. It may simply be that you have the wrong mix of skills or of personality types in your team. There may simply be too many personality conflicts.

Judging when to switch from mentoring team members, in the hope that they can step up to the mark, to taking the necessary action to move them elsewhere in the organisation or out of it altogether is one of the greatest challenges of management. The principle to bear in mind, of course, is that the team as an entity is far more important than any single individual in it. Inadequate or disruptive behaviour that frustrates the team's quest to achieve the goals set out in this chapter and Chapter Six ultimately has to be dealt with by the team leader.

Just as one of the team leader's natural instincts is to protect the members of their team to the point where this instinct may obstruct constructive disagreement, so it will tend to be the leader's instinct to give non-performing team members the benefit of the doubt for longer than is desirable. Most people tend to have an instinctive dislike of conflict. You know that your own emotions will often be heightened when dealing with poor performance and that those you are criticising may react in an emotional way towards you. So you tend to avoid conflict until it becomes untenable. But if you develop the discipline of dealing with issues as soon as they surface, you rarely have to deal with problematic emotions. I find it effective to ask the simple question: 'How do you think things are going?' I pause for as long as it takes to get the person to open up. Generally, it will bring to the fore everything you need to discuss.

It will be apparent that many of the team leadership skills discussed in this chapter concern helping your team members to understand themselves, and to become more aware of their strengths and weaknesses, and indeed of what they like and don't like doing. The best way of moving a square peg out of a round hole and into the right-sized square hole in the organisation is to help that peg understand its own shape and size and thus where it best fits. Enabling team members willingly to volunteer to move from an unsuitable role is the best result. Suggesting that they should move to a more suitable role and accomplishing that transition is the second-best result. Requiring them to move out of the organisation is the least desirable result, but is sometimes necessary for the overall interests of the team.

It is generally preferable to grow talent inside an organisation and to promote internally where possible (more on this in Chapter Eight). Internal candidates are better-known quantities than external candidates, reducing the risk involved in their appointment. They will already be steeped in the organisation's culture and will understand what it does and how it works. Internal promotion gives the signal to other colleagues that good performance will be rewarded and that those opportunities exist for others.

However, in part because of these benefits, many organisations create problems for themselves by placing staff in inappropriate roles, or over-promoting them to roles which they are not yet capable of fulfilling. These errors are then often exacerbated by not providing proper or effective training for these new roles. Where it is within your power as team leader, it is far better to bring in new talent as part of a properly managed and assessed recruitment process, than to push an existing team member into a role for which they are not ready. A promotion may seem like a favour at the time, but if it goes wrong it will rapidly turn into a great disservice.

If it does become necessary to part company with a member of your team, it is important that the process is handled with fairness and sensitivity. The individual concerned will inevitably be bruised and upset, but must be allowed to maintain their dignity at all times. The reasons for the departure will normally be apparent to the other members of the team but should nevertheless be clearly explained to the whole team by the team leader. If anyone believes that a former teammate has been unfairly or inhumanely treated, your progress towards elite status will be hindered or halted.

If you set clear standards and act fairly and consistently, it is rare that you will be challenged on removing an underperforming team member. Proper treatment means that individuals will leave with their pride intact. An elite team requires some turnover to ensure that it does not become stale or complacent. And as an organisation grows and develops, some internal skills will be inadequate, however hard people try to train and improve, and may need to be replaced from outside.

Leadership of a team inside other teams

Of course, many people in most medium-sized and large organisations act in a dual role – as the leader of one team, and as a member of another.

If the culture of the organisation to which you belong is not right, it is very hard to change it from the bottom or the middle. Effective cultural change in an organisation comes from the individuals who lead that organisation. That is what Chapter Eight is about.

In order to reach the upper echelons of an organisation in order to change it for the better, it is tempting to sink into the cultural errors that you want to change. It becomes tempting to play the game, to devote energy to office politics, to focus on being seen to do the right thing rather than doing it. Doing so is short-sighted. It means that by the time you get to the top, you run the risk of having forgotten why you wanted to get there in the first place. If the pole is greasy, and you try to climb it in the traditional way, by the time you get to the top you will be covered in grease. Grease is difficult to wash off.

At the start of your career you get promoted on the strength of your own specific competency and skills. As you progress, your further progress depends more and more on the impact you have on the people under you. Applying the principles described in this chapter and Chapter Six, however alien to the culture of the organisation of which you are part, means that the people around you will do better, and you will do better as a result. We've come back full circle to the start of Chapter Six and why you can achieve more as part of a team than on your own.

Training conflicts

In the middle of my career I was given a tough job. I was put in charge of training a Special Forces group of Territorial (part-time) soldiers to go to a major conflict area. The role I was to get them ready for was even tougher. They were to be posted to some of the most dangerous areas of the country to act as liaison officers between warring factions and other military units. They would be isolated in small teams of twelve, with very poor communications. They would be at considerable personal risk, and if they did not do their jobs properly and the relationship with the warlords broke down as a result, they would be putting many other soldiers at risk too. These soldiers were of a very high calibre. They had passed through an extremely rigorous selection process. But by definition, being part-time the Territorials have less time to hone their skills than the Regulars. My job was to get their training and skills up to Regular Special Forces standards, and I had just a few months to do it.

To help me, I had a team of eight Regulars. We started off by setting some very clear objectives and devised a very demanding training programme to get us there. Everyone was clear that if they did not meet the required standards within the set time they would be taken out of the programme. We trained, placing the Territorials under great pressure and testing them on a continuous basis against the rigorous standards we had set. A few did not get there and fell out along the way, but overall I was delighted with their commitment and progress. The message that I had delivered that no shortfall in standards would be tolerated had been clearly understood and had had its desired effect.

Six weeks into the programme I was called away for a weekend. The Territorials were due to carry out a two-day exercise and I left, confident that I would get a good report about them from the Regulars when I returned. Instead I got an urgent call from my second-in-command the second afternoon I was away. The news was not good. The trainees seemed to have forgotten everything they had learned so painstakingly over the previous weeks. They were behaving like rank amateurs, carrying out ambushes in the wrong places, making basic map-reading errors, and many other boy-soldier mistakes. They had regressed to raw cadets. As a result, morale had collapsed and each team was riven by recriminations.

I hurried back for a detailed report. The regular training team wanted to sack half the reserves because they had missed all our goals and the reserve soldiers had suffered a breakdown in their own command structure. I heard them all out but did not agree with any of them. I realised that I had made a mistake and had not delegated enough of the relationships with the trainees to my team. I'd built up the trust of the Territorials, but the motivation that drove their performance was too dependent on their relationship with me. I told my team that I planned to call them all together, switch some of the teams around and give them a second chance. My team did not all agree with me, but accepted that it was my decision and agreed to back me.

When I called everyone together for a debrief, having reorganised the teams and demoted one individual, I asked them to tell me what had gone wrong. Letting them talk made them all feel guilty. Their body language expressed their self-dissatisfaction; they shuffled their feet and looked around the room, avoiding eye contact. They knew they had let themselves down.

We now started by rebuilding the foundation of trust. We clarified the strengths and weaknesses of the current programme. We talked about the make-up of the teams and how we could adapt them. I spoke from the heart not only about my disappointment with the weekend but about my unquestionable belief in their ability to achieve great success. I also reminded them that a number of groups outside expected them to fail.

'If you continue like this,' I said, 'you surely won't disappoint our critics. We are not playing games here; this training is just as important as the job itself because if you do not do it properly you will not be able to do the job properly either. But I know you can meet the levels of performance we need. I am putting my reputation on the line for you because I know you can do it. But if there are any more mistakes – even the smallest mistake – you will be removed from the programme on the spot.'

We left the briefing with every team leader and team member absolutely clear about their roles and responsibilities. They understood that one of these roles was to hold each other to account. The required team results were also clearly articulated and we commenced the final two weeks of deployment training. Every one of them finished the training course successfully. Ultimately, they did a great job to the point where all of the regular soldiers and those who had initially been critical of the programme praised their performance. They completely and utterly justified my faith in them.

So what?

If you have mastered the art of being a good team member, becoming an effective team leader is likely to be a short step. This is because you will already understand the behaviour that makes an elite team. Whether team member or team leader, you are the same person. It would be wrong to try to change yourself; it is right to retain your authenticity.

If the team whose leader you become already understands and lives by the principles of the Circle of Elite Team Behaviour, your task will be an easy one. If they have not yet progressed to this point, you will have work to do. As you tease out the issues in your team, ensure that you demonstrate your own continued adherence to the principles of the Circle. Remain open; stay willing to expose your own vulnerabilities because, far from undermining your position, continuing to show common trust to your team will enhance your authority.

Demonstrate to your team that you hold team interests above your own by taking the blame yourself for any mistakes they make, but deal decisively and rapidly with inadequate team members once it is clear that they cannot adapt to the necessary behaviour. Because your team will hold each other to account, they will themselves start doing many of the internal aspects of your job, freeing you to focus your energies externally to your benefit and above all to the benefit of the team as a whole.

CHAPTER EIGHT

You as an organisational leader

To lead people, walk beside them … As for the best leaders, the people do not notice their existence. The next best, people honour and praise. The next, the people fear, and the next, the people hate … When the best leader's work is done, the people say, 'We did it ourselves.'

Lhao Shzu

'Behind enemy lines'

'As soon as the aircraft pulled away, Delta Eight moved out, getting away from the rendezvous site as fast as possible just in case any enemy had picked up the plane's noise and movement. Once in a safe location Tom called a halt to look at the information in the manila envelope. He then called his comrades together for a briefing.

'"There's another patrol out here. Stan, Jim and their lot. Call sign Delta Nine. They fired up a short-range radio so it looks as if they are in trouble. They're on foot. No vehicles. It's our job to find them and then get the hell out."

"How far off?" The expression on Kevin's face was very serious. There is nothing worse than learning that colleagues – friends – may be in difficulty.

"That last comms was seventy kilometres pretty much due west of here."

"So if we push it, we should be there around first light. What are we waiting for?"

'Tom did not smile at Colin's earnest eagerness. "I want to make sure that you all know what we are doing and why, and that you don't have any better ideas. We need to get over there quickly, but without taking any risks with the vehicles. If we break an axle it's not going to do anyone any good. Once we are over there we'll recce and make our plans then. Okay?"

'"Why can't they send in a plane?" asked Geordie.

'"No regular comms. Their signal could mean anything. May be hostiles in the area. We know they've got anti-aircraft missiles. It's too risky for a plane, and we are here. Okay?"

'This time he was answered by a unanimous chorus of quiet 'okays'.

'The night drive passed quickly. As before, the Delta Eight team took turns behind the wheel. The weather remained bitterly cold, with flurries of sleet driving into their faces because the east wind was exacerbated by the forward movement of the Land Rovers. Open military Land Rovers have no windscreen, of course. A grey, cloud-filtered light was touching the horizon behind them when Mick, who was navigating, leant over to Tom.

'"I reckon we are two kilometres away from their last known position." Tom raised his hand and the two Pinkies pulled up side by side. All the men scanned the surrounding desert, taking in the lie of the land.

'"See that higher ground over there?" Steve pointed to a scree-strewn slope two hundred metres to the north. "Why don't I recce up to the top and see what I can see?"

'"Makes sense. You may want to establish a position up there, so take Wings with you. Wings, you take the sniper rifle; you are handiest with it. Then if it makes sense, you can stay up there and cover us."

'These long-range sniper rifles, by the way, are accurate at up to a kilometre or more in the right hands. They can strike panic into the heart of an enemy because they pack a real punch and their sudden accuracy comes as a real shock.

'Steve and Wings set off up the slope as fast as the loose scree would allow and passed out of sight of the two vehicles.

Meanwhile, Colin tried to raise Delta Nine on the short-range Patrol Net radio. "Delta Nine, Delta Nine, this is Delta Eight, come in please, over."

'The radio crackled into life. "Delta Eight, I read you. Where are you? Over."

'Colin could not stifle a broad grin of relief. Tom took the microphone. "Location and sitrep [situation report] Delta Nine, please. Over."

'A map reference followed. Mick immediately identified it on the map as a knoll a little over a kilometre to the east. "We had enemy contact last night. They caught us in open ground and we had to dump our heavy kit. We are holed up in a good defensive position but surrounded by a mobile company strength force [approximately 100 people]. We gave them a bit of a pasting in the dark last night and I reckon they are waiting till it's light to make their next move. Over."

'"Any wounded? Over."

'"Yes." There was a pause. "We are all bloody freezing and Chico's in a pretty bad way – shot in the shoulder. Our ammo is limited too. Over."

'"Just hang on there. We'll work out the best way and come in to get you. You know what to expect. Out."

'Steve now came haring down the hill. "They're in the next valley. Surrounded but in a good position on a kind of isolated hill. Plenty of cover; I found them hard to spot. Enemy strength I'd estimate at a company; two of those jeeps we've already seen mounted with heavy machine guns, and four trucks."

'Steve's report was interrupted by the sound of gunfire from over the ridge in front.

'"Right, it's started. Get back up to Wings with Mick – that looks like the best fire support position. The four of us'll go in with the Pinkies and get as close to Delta Nine's position as we can. Don't disable the enemy trucks. We want to leave them the option to run. Start firing as soon as you get up there. Take out the two jeeps first. Wings'll know to target any officers he can identify. Usual drill. Let's go." Tom leapt behind the wheel of the first Land

Rover, followed by Kevin, Geordie and Colin, all moving instinctively to their positions with practised speed.

'By the time Steve and Mick reached Wings' position the enemy had fanned out in the valley over the ridge and started to move forward to try to get a foothold on Delta Nine's hilltop. The two jeeps had moved towards the bottom of the hill and were laying down ferocious fire on Delta's Nine's position.

'Even over the noise of his Land Rover, Tom heard the bark of the sniper rifle – deeper and somehow more decisive than the rattle of the automatic rifles. The volume of enemy fire suddenly reduced, and he knew that Wings had taken out the machine gunner in one of the jeeps. A second bark followed with the same effect.

'From the top of the hill the fire support team could see the panic their fire was spreading among the enemy. Wings carefully selected one target after another, supported by the more widely spread fire from Steve and Mick's machine guns. Then they saw the Pinkies hurtle over the lowest part of the ridge and down into the valley, pouring accurate fire onto the enemy positions. Without needing any more encouragement, the enemy soldiers turned and ran for the nearest covered trucks. Engines gunned and revved and the trucks drove as fast as they could the opposite way out of the valley.

'The eight members of Delta Nine emerged from their cover and scrambled down the hill towards the Pinkies. Stan was half-carrying Chico down the slope. They piled into the Land Rovers, which turned round to head back over the ridge the way they had come, pausing to pick up the fire support team on the way.

'"Sorry guys – it's a hell of a squash, but at least it will warm you up!" said Tom from behind the wheel.'

†

'Good to great'

Jim Collins' *Good to Great* is one of the most influential business books of modern times. In part this is because its findings are rooted not in opinion, but in scientific research. For the book, researchers looked back over forty years at the operating results of 1,435 established companies. From this large database, eleven were identified whose cumulative shareholder returns had outperformed the general stock market most strongly over a long period of time – fifteen years. To make the cut, the level of outperformance was 6.9 times. The list of these elite performers is perhaps not what you would expect: Abbott Laboratories, Circuit City, Fannie Mae, Gillette, Kimberley-Clark, Kroger, Nucor, Philip Morris, Pitney Bowes, Walgreens and Wells Fargo. Some are well-known names (male readers may well be rubbing their jaws thoughtfully right now and thinking, 'Yes, that was a close shave this morning'), but, if asked to name the strongest corporate performers, most people would be likely to come up with a completely different list.

Collins then analysed this elite group of eleven to work out the common features that contributed to each company's success. You will be pleased to hear that these features dovetail remarkably accurately with what has gone before in *Elite!*

Collins' first feature: leadership

Unsurprisingly, the first feature is leadership style. The characteristics of leaders in the 'good to great' companies – what Collins calls 'Level 5 leadership' – mirror the qualities of team leadership that I advocate in Chapter Seven: ambition for the success of the organisation rather than themselves, self-effacing characteristics that enable them to allow their team to take the credit and help them to develop their successors, and a ferocious resolve to achieve excellence. I cannot better Collins' own words:

> Level 5 leaders look out of the window to apportion credit to factors outside themselves when things go well (and if they cannot find a specific person or event to give credit to, they credit good luck). At the same time, they look in the mirror to apportion responsibility, never blaming bad luck when things go poorly (p. 35).

Feature 2: the right people doing the right jobs

The second theme is these companies' focus on having the right people in the organisation and then deciding what to do, or as Collins says: 'First "who", then "what". Many concerns do it the other way round; they develop their vision and strategy, and then set about recruiting the people to execute them. Often the vision and strategy are embodied in one charismatic leader, which in itself makes the institution vulnerable. It also means that the team is recruited to implement a strategy and vision that belongs to someone else. The 'good to great' companies concentrate first on making sure that they have the best people in the right places in their organisation. Then they use the skills of those people to help develop their plan. Because of the quality of the team, there is a higher chance of choosing the right direction, and because the team has developed the plan itself there will be far more commitment to it. When I left the military after my twenty-seven years as a soldier, the group I had been part of continued to develop and grow. I enjoyed their expressions of thanks, but the greatest thanks of all was the way that others stepped into my role and continued with the culture and ethos that had gone before.

Another feature of the way that 'good to great' companies build their team is that much promotion is internal. They tend to invest more in staff training and development and thus have to go outside for recruitment less. This applies also to the selection of their leader; in many cases the CEO who exemplifies and perpetuates the 'good to great' culture is home grown. This strikes a particular chord with me, because this is the way we do things in the military too.

But when, as is sometimes necessary, candidates have to be sought outside the organisation, 'good to great' companies act swiftly and decisively. I hope that this all sounds familiar from my Chapter Seven.

And when you have good people you have to use them correctly, focusing the best on the biggest opportunities, not the biggest problems, making sure that the important issues are debated vigorously in the search for the correct answer. Remember positive disagreement and the primacy of the team from the Circle of Elite Team Behaviour? Again, I have to quote Jim Collins: 'Good-to-great management teams consist of people who debate vigorously in search of the best answers, yet who unify behind decisions, regardless of parochial interests' (p. 63).

I hope that sounds familiar.

Feature 3: objective analysis

This third feature really follows on from the vigorous debate that characterises positive disagreement. Great leaders ask great questions. Too many leaders start by assuming they have the answers, or are afraid to show weakness by suggesting that they might not have the answers. In fact, asking the right questions in order to understand the true facts is one of the tell-tale signs of a strong leader.

One of the corollaries of asking the right questions is that the realities of the marketplace will be confronted. Organisations that are led in the wrong way risk ignoring the harsh competitive realities of the world around them. Sometimes in large organisations you find middle managers who will say, 'This is what we've been told to do, but the boss just does not understand what we are up against', or words to that effect. These middle managers will be flat, demotivated, and are unlikely to succeed. Acknowledging a challenge and really understanding it are the first steps towards overcoming it. A challenge that is recognised, understood and rehearsed becomes far less frightening than one that you are too scared to confront. With the right attitude and mental toughness, it is possible to maintain an absolute belief in ultimate victory without denying the difficulties inherent in achieving that success.

Don't be an ostrich. Great leaders only stick their heads in the sand to see what might be wriggling about underneath the surface that they need to deal with, not to hide from reality. Or, to mix my clichés, they don't sweep rubbish under the carpet; they lift up the carpet to check what might be there that needs cleaning up, however unpleasant that might be.

Feature 4: focus

The fourth 'good to great' feature in Jim Collins' six he calls the 'hedgehog concept'. In my terms, this is focus: identifying the one thing at which you really can excel and concentrating on it, ensuring that you have the skills and the tools to achieve the elite performance you need in your area. Remember that in a 'good to great' organisation the choice of focus is not just yours as leader. The choice of focus is made by the organisation after open and vigorous debate. In this way the vision and direction of the organisation belongs to the whole team, and its achievement becomes a common passion.

Collins points out that in a substantial organisation it may take time to identify the 'hedgehog concept' and advocates using a 'business council', a group of half a dozen to a dozen key executives in the organisation who meet regularly to discuss and debate the issues it faces.

Feature 5: discipline

Collins' number five is building a culture of discipline throughout the organisation. I hope you recognise this as a theme that has run through all the chapters of this book. True discipline is not about imposing authority tyrannically from above. That is not how we do things in the Regiment, or how things are done in any elite organisation whether Special Forces or not. The right culture of discipline actually allows considerable freedom in the organisation, within clearly explained and understood boundaries of course, inside which individuals have responsibility themselves, coupled with the self-discipline to exercise that responsibility to the greatest benefit of the organisation as a whole. This type of discipline is self-policing and reduces the need for bureaucracy, which is often imposed to compensate for incompetence and carelessness. It also becomes self-perpetuating and acts as the backbone of an organisation.

To quote Jim Collins once more:

> It all starts with disciplined *people*. The transition begins not by trying to discipline the wrong people into the right behaviors, but by getting *self*-disciplined people on the bus in the first place. Next we have disciplined *thought*. You need the discipline to confront the brutal facts of reality, while retaining resolute faith that you can and will create a path to greatness. Most importantly, you need the discipline to persist in the search for understanding until you get to your Hedgehog Concept. Finally, we have disciplined *action* … This order is important. The comparison companies often tried to jump right to disciplined action. But disciplined action without self-disciplined people is impossible to sustain, and disciplined action without disciplined thought is a recipe for disaster. (p. 126)

Discipline has always been one of the power words I use to maintain my focus.

Feature 6: using technology correctly

Collins' sixth and final point relates to the way these 'good to great' companies use technology to further the aims of their business. He calls it 'Technology accelerator'. Rather than adopting a new technology for the sake of it – just because that is what other organisations around them are doing – they ask whether the new technology fits with what they are focusing on. If it doesn't, they don't use it; if it does, they pioneer it and often use it in a unique and original way. This intelligent use of new technology, or new techniques, can accelerate an organisation and catapult it forward.

From team member, to team leader, to organisational leader

Just as the transition from team member to team leader should be a natural progression, so should the transition be from team leader to organisational leader, or the leadership of several teams. The same principles apply. Never lose sight of the four points on the Circle of Elite Team Behaviour.

In some ways, as you rise towards the top of the organisation it becomes easier because of the decline in the number of influences pressing down on you from above, which may be at odds with your vision and your knowledge about how to achieve elite performance. There is less chance of someone above you in the organisation imposing a different culture downwards in a dictatorial, non-elite way, and of preventing you from doing what you know needs to be done.

In other ways, though, it becomes more challenging. As you move up an organisation, you inevitably become more remote from the coalface, and it can become harder to understand what is going on. The view from the top of the mountain is wider and broader. You can see further. But you can no longer see the detail of what is happening in the thickets at the bottom where you started your climb.

And that position at the top of the mountain can be cold and windy, and will become lonely if you allow it to. Don't do it like Moses. Don't go to the top of the mountain by yourself, hang around up there receiving revelations, and then charge back down to the bottom, find out that something has gone wrong in your absence and go ballistic with rage. Remember your team; take them to the top of the mountain with you and stay connected. Continue to work with your direct reports in the way that you learnt in Chapter Seven, when you were just a team leader. Make sure that your immediate team stay connected with their teams in the same way, and so on right down to the bottom of the mountain.

Communication

Of course, at more senior levels in an organisation you will tend to have to take on more responsibility for communicating with larger groups, for example addressing sales conferences or company-wide meetings. There is a delicate balance to get right here. On the one hand, you need to demonstrate to these audiences why you have the skills and talents to be the leader; on the other hand, you must make clear repeatedly the team culture of the organisation and demonstrate that the primacy of the team is paramount and that its achievements are collective achievements, not just yours. Remember that the first feature of 'good to great' companies is that they do not have loud, charismatic leaders who build a personality cult and become household names. Give credit; don't take credit. When you bang the drum, make sure it is the team drum, not your personal drum. And get the other members of your team to bang the drum with you. Your objective must be to be seen as *'primus inter pares'* – first amongst equals, not as some stand-out figurehead.

And don't forget Chapter Five and your own training. Take time to perfect the new communication skills you will need for your senior role. This is one of the basics you need to get right.

Information

You also need to make sure you understand what is going on in your organisation. Of course, that does not mean obsessively chasing down every scrap of management information and burying yourself under a mound of data. If you have worked out what sort of hedgehog your organisation is, you will also have worked out what metrics really matter, and which data really tells you whether you are succeeding in your focus. It is far better to concentrate on a small number of pieces of management information through which you can follow and understand patterns and trends than to become mired in a mass of detail. Too often I have seen even talented managing directors delve so far down into the detail that they create an environment of mistrust. If their direct reports come to feel that they are being checked up on, they will interpret this behaviour as a lack of confidence. The managing directors who behave in this way generally do not have time for strategy because they immerse themselves in the operational and tactical detail. Inevitably this inability to delegate properly is very limiting behaviour and throws doubt on their suitability for the highest levels of an organisation.

From time to time it is obviously important to descend from the summit of your mountain to observe directly what is happening on its flanks and lower slopes, and even in those thickets right at the bottom. When you do so, make sure that you are down to earth and approachable, but that you do not undermine the authority of those who have immediate responsibility for the thickets by accepting or implying criticism of the way they are running things. Having reached the top of the mountain does not give you the right not to work through the correct channels.

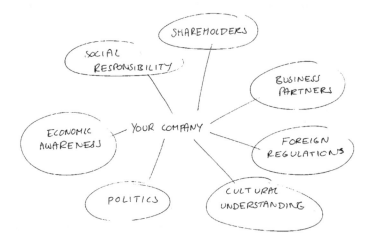

ORGANISATIONAL LEADERSHIP IS ABOUT BECOMING AWARE OF ALL THE SYSTEMS THAT AFFECT YOUR ROLE

Working with stakeholders outside your organisation

Another characteristic of your position at the summit or on the upper slopes of an organisation is that more of your role is likely to be about looking outwards. You will have to spend more time dealing with external partners, customers, shareholders, industry associations, perhaps civil servants and politicians. These will all be entities over which you have no direct control, or limited control at best. Their culture may be radically different from the elite culture that you have instilled in your own organisation. Some may be downright hostile, and some may have objectives that conflict with yours. Even when the objectives are theoretically aligned, you may encounter hostility and suspicion.

Some of the lessons I have tried to impart in Chapter Four on communication and negotiation are obviously relevant here. But it also becomes necessary to approach the process of negotiation in a more strategic way, working out from a range of possibilities who the best probable partners are likely to be and how to influence them most effectively. A frontal assault may not be most effective; it may be better to influence and win as an ally a different group who can then help you to attain your goal.

Strategic collaboration

One of the most challenging tasks I faced soon after leaving the military was in the world of counter-terrorism overseas. I was tasked with training a senior leadership team to ensure that they were equipped to deal with all types of terrorist incident. I quickly saw that this team was highly competent and already well trained. There was little I could teach them about their own roles. The real challenge was that I could not achieve the objective just by training my team. They did not have ultimate authority for counter-terrorist incidents; theirs was a supporting role. Meeting the terrorist challenge effectively required the co-operation of a whole string of organisations – police forces, SWAT teams, various military units, Intelligence Services and several government departments. I needed them all to work and train alongside one another, but I had no authority to require them to do so. What is more, it rapidly became apparent that these groups were riddled with mutual suspicion and hostility. They had different cultures, operating procedures and KPIs. They also distrusted my own motives and felt threatened by the proposals I made for them to work together in a more co-ordinated way.

It was clear that this project would take at least three years. We needed that amount of time to ensure that we had worked in all of the key regions and tested the working practices of each group. So whilst training the team for which I was directly responsible to be as prepared as possible to deal with any terrorist situation that might occur, I searched for like minds in each of the key regions. I managed to identify a commander of one region who did understand the threat that a terrorist incident posed and was willing to admit that his group was ill-prepared at command, operational and tactical levels to deal with it.

I needed to form an alliance with a senior decision-maker. Here was one with humility and a desire to stretch his leadership team to the full – a desire for his team to achieve elite status. It took us just two months to set up an exercise together. In doing so, we were challenging conventional wisdom and going against decades of old training models that were ineffective, time-consuming and resource-intensive. It was essential to have an early success to prove to the other stakeholders that my new approach was the correct format to use.

As with any effective training exercise, the key objective was to make the whole exercise as close to the real thing as possible. We planned a five-day exercise, with the first two days focused on developing specific skill sets to ensure interoperability between the groups who would work on the project. This meant that we had government officials working alongside police and military units who would be tasked with bringing any incident under control. The following two days were spent putting those skills under pressure with a string of very short exercises. This meant that the units on the ground would understand how to adapt to many different eventualities, that the field commanders would learn to make difficult decisions on the ground at a tactical and operational level, and that the senior commanders would understand how to make strategic decisions in their command centres.

Once we had run through these elements, on day five they were tested in a demanding exercise during which everyone's capabilities were assessed. No external support was given so that the exercise ran and adapted to the decisions that were made by the people who would be responsible in real life.

Because of this format the exercise was as close to the real thing as one could possibly get. If an individual made a decision on the ground and it was wrong, there was no going back. All the teams had to live with it. The pressure was tangible.

There was another sort of pressure too, because I invited representatives from all the other regions to come and watch what happened.

The exercise was a huge success because those involved really placed themselves on the line. They came to realise that they were capable of performing at an elite level. Within three years we had taken the same training formula to every region of the country.

Two years later, I learned that a major terrorist incident had occurred which required these groups to work together in three different regions. When they came to deal with this real-life incident they could not believe how simple it was after the complexity of the training they had completed.

Another important strength to master is the ability to look beyond short-term pressures to concentrate on what is necessary for medium- and long-term success. Pressure to perform in the short term and to deliver immediate results can be acute, whether driven by stock market pressure or other considerations. Often it mitigates against elite – or 'good to great' – performance, which is best measured over a longer period. When I first started working with business leaders, I was often surprised at the lack of training they had had and the difficulty they faced in moving from short-term to medium-term to long-term thinking. Of course, many business leaders are driven to deliver results on a quarterly cycle, but without the ability to look ahead and put the correct strategy in place they will constantly come up short.

Stand up and be counted

One of the best CEOs that I have been privileged to coach ran a national sports team (I learnt just as much from him as he did from me). He had multiple stakeholders to deal with, many with personal or regional goals at odds with his national perspective. The success of the team on the international stage was a paramount objective, as was building the commercial business associated with the team. Sporting success would bring commercial success, and the profits from that commercial success could then be used to fuel more sporting success.

I watched this CEO work with his team to develop a strategy that would take six years to be fully realised and then saw him undertake the most intense negotiations to bring not only the external stakeholders with him but also some of the internal stakeholders as well. He carried this out in a cauldron of pressure, under media fire, with very few people supporting him initially, and many longing for him not to succeed. The word that stands out in this situation is *courage*.

He held firm on his long-term strategy and achieved a number of small, carefully planned successes. Each of these provided a base for the next and formed a step on the way towards his final vision of the internationally successful team coupled with a profitable commercial enterprise. Applying the principles of the Circle of Elite Team Behaviour, he brought his leadership team along with him and won the support of most of the external and internal stakeholders. Some of the stakeholders may remain unhappy because they have lost control and influence (you have to be aware that you will hardly ever capture everyone), but they cannot deny that this organisation is a force in their sport and one of the most commercially viable ones at that. I am confident that if they remain on course they will have a decade of success ahead of them.

Succession

Perhaps the ultimate test of an elite leader is how effectively they put themself out of a job. Remember that the elite leader is focused on the primacy of the team, not on their own narrow career interest. At the forefront of an elite leader's mind, therefore, will be succession planning.'Who is going to take over when I go? When should that be?' Often the answer to that second question is: 'When someone else is ready to do the job as well as or better than I can.' An elite leader will not try to hold on to their position beyond the point at which the organisation or the team can benefit more from different leadership.

And the truly elite leader will possess the self-awareness to judge correctly when that time comes. Their real reward will come from the respect and awe with which they are remembered as a result of taking those decisions that put the team first.

So what?

The most important characteristic of an elite leader of an organisation is humility. If the man or the woman at the top of the pile demonstrates genuinely and authentically that the organisation is more important than its leader, they are well on the way to instilling the right culture and thus securing their own success. There is no better way to engender loyalty than to allow your team to take the credit for things that go right and to take the blame yourself for those that go wrong.

Always try to hire individuals who are more talented and more able than you are. Nothing is more important than getting the right people into your organisation. Most people who are really good at what they do are humble, because their knowledge of their ability creates self-confidence and reduces the need for external adulation. But if the potential recruit does suffer from arrogance and will not perpetuate the culture and the discipline you want throughout the organisation, do not take them on however talented they may be.

215

Your humility will make you an approachable leader without undermining your subordinates' authority. Your approachability will enable you to maintain a variety of communication channels so that, coupled with your focus on the information that is most important, you will really know what is going on. It is often said that great leaders are the ones who do themselves out of a job through careful succession-planning and knowing when to step down; in an elite organisation this is far easier to do because the cells that make it up are healthy and self-sustaining.

CHAPTER NINE

Conclusions

Men are not afraid of things, but of how they view them.

Epictetus

If you are pained by external things, it is not they that disturb you, but your own judgement of them. And it is in your power to wipe out that judgement now.

Marcus Aurelius

'Behind enemy lines'

'So the thirteen of them got back safely?'

'Yes – basically they drove south as quickly as they could. They judged that travelling in daylight was less risky than hanging around. They were right – they made it back without further incident.'

'And Martin?'

'Martin – and Chico – recovered fully. Both were pretty tough guys, and the team's quick action in getting them back for proper medical treatment gave them the best possible chance.'

'So I guess Delta Nine had pretty bad luck then.'

Floyd leaned forward at my comment, and I began to feel uncomfortable. His unwavering gaze seemed to be drilling a hole into the middle of my forehead, just above the top of my nose.

'I'm sorry; did I say something wrong?' Somehow Floyd had wrenched the expression of contrition out of my mouth, almost without my being aware of speaking.

He relaxed, sat back again and smiled. I relaxed too.

'Well, yes, you did actually. Bad luck, you said. Luck? Luck does not come into it. We are in control of our own destinies, not at the whim of some force of fate. Sure, external circumstances have an impact on us, but we respond to those circumstances. Our planning takes into account what may happen, and our training prepares us to handle whatever comes. No, Delta Nine didn't have bad luck. They planned and prepared less well than they should have. They did not fulfil their potential as an elite team. They made mistakes. They won't again. Their debrief helped them to realise where they could enhance their performance next time. There would have been some passionate and heated debate, of course, but it was respectful. What is more, other units would have learned from Delta Nine's mistakes because those lessons would have been disseminated to other patrols.

'You see, when we are performing at elite levels, the margin for error is wafer-thin. Delta Nine weren't bad at what they did. Nobody in the Regiment, past or present, is bad at what they do. When they were in the field they performed with great courage and skill. One or two of their decisions were sub-optimal and they missed a couple of chances to put things right.

'It's true that the mix of the Delta Nine team was unfortunate. The two senior guys, Jim the sergeant and Stan the corporal, were identical personalities – outgoing, perhaps even domineering. Those characteristics were fed by Billy and Chico, two of the new guys, who were themselves very similar. Their view of Jim and Stan came uncomfortably close to hero worship and really exacerbated the problem.

'The three experienced guys – Stu, Fletch and Evan – were best placed to bring some balance to the team. But they were really far over at the introvert end of the scale. They weren't totally happy with the plan and they really should have pushed their views forward. Jim's efforts to involve them were half-hearted, partly because he was playing to the gallery of Billy and Chico a bit too much. He should have pressed them harder for their opinions. And he shouldn't have allowed himself to slap down Gus, the other younger guy, when he did, even if Gus's way of expressing himself was out of order. Stan nearly saved the day, but left it too late.'

'Yes,' I chipped in, 'I'm sure I've read somewhere the phrase "Disciplined action without disciplined thought is a recipe for disaster".'

Floyd smiled and carried on.'In some ways, if you allow yourself to use the words "bad luck", Delta Eight had more of it than Delta Nine. You could say it was "bad luck" that Martin was shot in the back in the first volley of enemy fire. Or you could say that one of the enemy knew how to shoot straight. Being hit, and your leader being hit, are things you have to be prepared for in combat, after all. And Delta Eight were prepared for it. They had made the right calls, and were in a position to react and pull their chestnuts out of the fire. They planned well and were ready for the conditions. They carried out the basics well because they'd practised until they became second nature. They trusted one another; they did not have to look left or right because they knew their teammates would be there. They held one another to account for their actions. In other words, in the pressure zone, in the red zone, they operated as an elite team. They'd given themselves the best chance of success.'

'Okay, I get it. If we can get all this stuff in the book, then I think it will be an interesting read!'

Floyd corrected me again, but with a smile this time. 'And useful, practically useful. That is the most important thing.'

✝

A final so what?

I hope that this book has been thought-provoking. I hope at least that it has challenged you to look at your own skills and behaviours. I hope that I may have pushed you further into the pressure zone.

I hope too that it has provided you with some really useful advice that you can put into practice in your career, whatever it may be.

The message that I really want to underline – the *Elite!* lesson if you like – is that *we can all achieve excellence in our chosen field*. All it requires is the structured approach that I have tried to explain in this book and the self-discipline and commitment to put it into practice.

I have always found it vital to understand my own performance first and then to understand the people around me. The first step towards elite behaviour must be to understand the principles behind it so that we can use them consistently as a compass for performance.

I have no doubt that the tools I have explained in the previous chapters will give you an edge. I believe that the most important element is where you started – the human mind and the fact that it will do what it is told to do by its owner. If there is one lesson to remember from this book, that is it. You are in control of yourself; you are in charge.

If you like the sound of the information in this book and think that it will help you but do not use it – nothing will change. How many times have you been on training courses where you come across great ideas and yet do not implement them? You simply go back to the stale old programs already in your mind. You forget to upgrade.

Nothing happens without commitment. You have to commit to improvement. You have to evolve. Nature is very cruel to those who do not evolve.

Before you started reading this book you may well have been doing many of the things it advocates. I hope that it will help you achieve success by clarifying your conscious understanding of the positive elements in your performance. Once you really understand these elements you can apply them to your individual performance. Only then can you apply them when you are working as a leader of a team or teams.

When I look back at my career, one thing that really stands out is that I have always been surrounded by talented people – and I still am. This has raised my own standards and made it that much easier to develop my own ability to lead and make good decisions. Excellence breeds excellence. Surrounding yourself with the right team is not easy, whether it means winning membership of a great team or bringing one together. But it is key to success.

It is the golden thread that closes the loop.

Personality profiling questionnaires available online

http://www.capt.org/take-mbti-assessment/mbti.htm

http://www.humanmetrics.com/cgi-win/jtypes2.asp

http://www.personalitypathways.com/type_inventory.html

http://www.teamtechnology.co.uk/mmdi/questionnaire/

http://kisa.ca/personality/

The British Army's *Principles of War*
Joint Defence Publication 0-01, British Defence Doctrine
(Fourth Edition), November 2011.

The British Army's *Principles of War* were first published after the First World War based on the work of J. F. C. Fuller. The definition of each principle has been refined over subsequent decades. They are adopted throughout the British armed forces. The tenth principle, added later, was originally called 'Administration'. The first principle has always been stated as pre-eminent and the second is usually considered more important than the remainder, which are not listed in any order of importance.

These principles of war are also commonly used by the armed forces of Commonwealth countries such as Australia. I often bring these into my business conversations because they are equally applicable with only a slight adaptation of the words and meaning.

The 2011 edition of the *British Defence Doctrine* explains the principles with the following preface:

> Principles of War guide commanders and their staffs in the planning and conduct of warfare. They are enduring, but not immutable, absolute or prescriptive, and provide an appropriate foundation for all military activity. The relative importance of each may vary according to context; their application requires judgement, common sense and intelligent interpretation. Commanders also need to take into account the legitimacy of their actions, based on the legal, moral, political, diplomatic and ethical propriety of the conduct of military forces, once committed.

The ten principles are:

1. *Selection and maintenance of the aim*: A single, unambiguous aim is the keystone of successful military operations. Selection and maintenance of the aim is regarded as the master principle of war.
2. *Maintenance of morale*: Morale is a positive state of mind derived from inspired political and military leadership, a shared sense of purpose and values, well-being, perceptions of worth and group cohesion.
3. *Offensive action*: Offensive action is the practical way in which a commander seeks to gain advantage, sustain momentum and seize the initiative.
4. *Security*: Security is the provision and maintenance of an operating environment that affords the necessary freedom of action, when and where required, to achieve objectives.
5. *Surprise*: Surprise is the consequence of shock and confusion induced by the deliberate or incidental introduction of the unexpected.
6. *Concentration of force*: Concentration of force involves the decisive, synchronised application of superior fighting power (conceptual, physical and moral) to realise intended effects, when and where required.
7. *Economy of effort*: Economy of effort is the judicious exploitation of manpower, material and time in relation to the achievement of objectives.
8. *Flexibility*: Flexibility – the ability to change readily to meet new circumstances – comprises agility, responsiveness, resilience, acuity and adaptability.
9. *Co-operation*: Co-operation entails the incorporation of teamwork and a sharing of dangers, burdens, risks and opportunities in every aspect of warfare.
10. *Sustainability*: To sustain a force is to generate the means by which its fighting power and freedom of action are maintained.

APPENDIX III

Further reading

Barr, L. and Barr, N. (1994). *Leadership Development: Maturity and power.* Waco, TX: Eakin Press.

Barrett, R. (2010). *The New Leadership Paradigm: A leadership development handbook for the twenty-first century leader.* Lulu. com.

Collins, J. (2001). *Good to Great: Why some companies make the leap ... and others don't.* New York: Random House Business.

Csíkszentmihályi, M. (1990). *Flow: The psychology of optimal experience.* New York: Harper and Row.

Curran, A. (2008). *The Little Book of Big Stuff about the Brain: The true story of your amazing brain,* ed. I. Gilbert. Carmarthen: Crown House Publishing.

Drucker, P. (2011). *Management Challenges for the 21st Century.* New York: HarperBusiness.

Goleman, D. (1998). *Working with Emotional Intelligence.* New York: Bantam Books.

Keirsey, D. (1998). *Please Understand Me II: Temperament, character, intelligence.* San Diego, CA: Prometheus Nemesis Book Company.

Lempereur, A. and Colson, A. (2010). *The First Move: A negotiator's companion,* ed. M. Pekar. Chichester: Wiley.

Lencioni, P. (2002). *The Five Dysfunctions of a Team: A leadership fable.* San Francisco, CA: Jossey Bass.

Pease, A. and Pease, B. (2011). *Body Language in the Workplace.* London: Orion.

Thorn, J. (2009). *How to Negotiate Better Deals.* Oxford: Management Books 2000.